> The joy of the series, of reading *Remote Control, Golf Ball, Driver's License, Drone, Silence, Glass, Refrigerator, Hotel,* and *Waste* . . . in quick succession, lies in encountering the various turns through which each of their authors has been put by his or her object. . . . The object predominates, sits squarely center stage, directs the action. The object decides the genre, the chronology, and the limits of the study. Accordingly, the author has to take her cue from the *thing* she chose or that chose her. The result is a wonderfully uneven series of books, each one a *thing* unto itself."

Julian Yates, *Los Angeles Review of Books*

> The Object Lessons series has a beautifully simple premise. Each book or essay centers on a specific object. This can be mundane or unexpected, humorous or politically timely. Whatever the subject, these descriptions reveal the rich worlds hidden under the surface of things."

Christine Ro, *Book Riot*

> . . . a sensibility somewhere between Roland Barthes and Wes Anderson."

Simon Reynolds, author of *Retromania: Pop Culture's Addiction to Its Own Past*

OBJECTLESSONS

A book series about the hidden lives of ordinary things.

Series Editors:

Ian Bogost and Christopher Schaberg

Advisory Board:

Sara Ahmed, Jane Bennett, Jeffrey Jerome Cohen, Johanna
Drucker, Raiford Guins, Graham Harman, renée hoogland,
Pam Houston, Eileen Joy, Douglas Kahn, Daniel Miller,
Esther Milne, Timothy Morton, Kathleen Stewart, Nigel
Thrift, Rob Walker, Michele White.

In association with

Georgia Tech | Center for Media Studies

BOOKS IN THE SERIES

coffee

DINAH LENNEY

BLOOMSBURY ACADEMIC
NEW YORK • LONDON • OXFORD • NEW DELHI • SYDNEY

BLOOMSBURY ACADEMIC
Bloomsbury Publishing Inc
1385 Broadway, New York, NY 10018, USA
50 Bedford Square, London, WC1B 3DP, UK

BLOOMSBURY, BLOOMSBURY ACADEMIC and the Diana logo are
trademarks of Bloomsbury Publishing Plc

First published in the United States of America 2020

Cover design: Alice Marwick

Bloomsbury Publishing Inc does not have any control over, or responsibility
for, any third-party websites referred to or in this book. All internet addresses given in
this book were correct at the time of going to press. The author and publisher regret any
inconvenience caused if addresses have changed or sites have ceased to exist, but can
accept no responsibility for any such changes.

Library of Congress Cataloging-in-Publication Data
Names: Lenney, Dinah, author.
Title: Coffee / Dinah Lenney.
Description: New York: Bloomsbury Academic, 2020. | Series: Object lessons
| Includes bibliographical references and index.
Identifiers: LCCN 2019040302 | ISBN 9781501344350 (paperback) |
ISBN 9781501344367 (epub) | ISBN 9781501344374 (pdf)
Subjects: LCSH: Coffee–Social aspects. | Friendship. | Coffee shops–Social aspects.
Classification: LCC GT2918 .L45 2020 | DDC 394.1/2–dc23
LC record available at https://lccn.loc.gov/2019040302

ISBN: PB: 978-1-5013-4435-0
ePDF: 978-1-5013-4437-4
eBook: 978-1-5013-4436-7

Series: Object Lessons

Typeset by Deanta Global Publishing Services, Chennai, India
Printed and bound in the United States of America

To find out more about our authors and books visit www.bloomsbury.com
and sign up for our newsletters.

How much better is silence; the coffee cup, the table.
How much better to sit by myself like the solitary sea-
bird that opens its wings on the stake. Let me sit here for
ever with bare things, this coffee cup, this knife, this fork,
things in themselves, myself being myself.

—VIRGINIA WOOLF, *THE WAVES*

CONTENTS

PROLOGUE

"Mornings are tough," writes a friend. And she's not the only one. Another, a woman I've known much longer, feels just the same: "Every day," she tells me, "I wake with such dread." A third insists coffee is the only reason—and she's not being funny or glib. "If not for coffee," she says, "I'd never get out of bed." Of course, some people don't get out of bed—some have their first cup delivered on a tray with a bud in a vase. Or just all by itself in a big friendly mug.

Nice work if you can get it, but it wouldn't work for me.

Zoom in from the sliding glass doors on a woman in her robe, and, depending on the season, very possibly socks, sliding from the sink to the stove (a wide shot, in the animated version): she loves that time, between turning up the flame under the kettle—and dampening the filter, and grinding and measuring the grounds, and breathing them in (tighter here, tight as possible, nose in the bag)—and the moment when the coffee is ready to pour.

Maybe, in those minutes, she—I—she is me, of course—maybe I take note of the color of the sky; maybe I grab for my phone to take a picture of the sun coming up through the leaves of the Chinese elm (the same picture again and again,

I keep taking it as if it will be different, as if I'll get it right); or maybe the counters need wiping—coffee dust here and there, also parmesan cheese from the previous evening, or a smear of red sauce, or a glisten of oil—

There is maybe laundry to get from the dryer, or a pile in a basket to fold—

There's checking Instagram, of course—then email, then Twitter (I've given up Facebook, except for Scrabble)—

Often, there's a puzzle on the long kitchen table: I might even manage a piece before I pour my first cup—

What I'm on about, though: I can hardly wait to get up in the morning. Not that I'm all bouncy about it. More likely swimming up from the dark, hoping to emerge without a ripple, trying to keep the feel of those watery dreams on my skin for as long as I can. I'm saying, I'm quiet getting out of bed, retrieving my robe, climbing the stairs. Morning is only my favorite time if I'm the only one up. I have to have it all to myself. Before a human has yet said a word—before *I've* said a word—the day, not discernibly begun, clear and unsullied, not a mark on it anywhere. (For me, the dread comes on later, as the hours clutter up with voices and tasks.)

Picture this, someone draw this for me:

A woman in her robe (in the cartoon she never takes it off), pushing a buzzing, throbbing, misshapen boulder of a day up a hill called Time, heaving it over the edge into night, falling backwards with the effort, and waking at the bottom again, with a pebble of a morning, bare, shimmering, on the table before her. And coffee.

1 THE IMPOSSIBILITY OF THE TASK

Some months ago I was virtually introduced to Dan McCloskey, who founded a company called Premium Quality Consulting.[1] He's spent "a lifetime in the coffee business," so says his bio on the website, and the company advises about all manner of industry concerns, local to global, from marketing, to branding, to wholesale operations. **Coffee consulting for your biggest challenges** [announces the homepage]**: what worries you most?**

"Dear Dan," I confided in an email just after a preliminary exchange. "Clearly, I've lost my mind." I explained that I was suddenly having trouble letting anyone else make the coffee. In my kitchen. For two. That just the other morning my husband went to pick up the kettle and I stopped him—rudely—

"Dinah," Fred said, "I think I know how to pour water."

And it's true, he does. Of course he does.

---

[1] Their slogan: "In the coffee business, we've done it. We're here for you."

Dan responded generously. As if I hadn't lost perspective, not to mention a sense of boundaries. (Thank you, Dan.) He referred to the ubiquity of coffees, the clichés, the frustrations ("it's described with tropes that don't add up to much under investigation"). Keep in mind, though, he added, "Six out of ten people drink coffee," and, new paragraph, he wrote, "[Coffee is] a common human experience that doesn't recognize identity, religion, culture, or position."

Reassuring, right? And true. Or if not entirely true (there are beans that sell for $50 to $500 a pound[2]—but who can buy those beans? Who *would*?), it should be.

Toward the end of his note, Dan said about coffee: "For me, there's nothing special or innocent left—except *every single day* when I wake up and have a cup. I rise up into consciousness thinking I can't possibly face the day and then I have a coffee, the adenosine flushes from my brain, and I'm myself again." (Note to self at the time: look up adenosine.[3])

"You won't solve coffee," Dan McCloskey wrote, "so don't fight the impossibility of the task . . ."

---

[2]Herewith, a list of ten coffees that go for more than 30 bucks a pound, including Black Ivory coffee, harvested from elephant poop, then roasted and bagged, no kidding around. https://financesonline.com/top-10-most-expensive-coffee-in-the-world-luwak-coffee-is-not-the-no-1/.

[3]A naturally occurring molecule produced when the body runs out of fuel. It makes a person want to sleep. Coffee counters that, but: the more coffee we drink, the more adenosine we produce. Too much coffee, too much adenosine, which makes it hard to wake up, which makes us want more coffee . . .

How deflating. I won't solve coffee. How to deal with the fact that I won't solve coffee? Or, extending the metaphor, anything else? And time running out, what to do, what next, how to be, why bother, oh no—despair. How to counter this sense of despair? With coffee, that's how. No really, I mean it, I do.

2 MY MOTHER IS COMING, MY MOTHER IS COMING

This, says my son, as if to a third party, as if we're not the only two in the room, *This* is a woman (so he has to be speaking to me about me) with a mother complex—

He says this because he hears me muttering to myself about putting the sheets through one more wash (because they're new! Because I want them to be soft!)—and because I'm fussing, moving a fern from one side of the room to the other and back—

Later, sheets still warm from the dryer, I call from the guest room. Does he want me to teach him to make hospital corners? Big surprise, he does not. "Everyone should know how to make hospital corners," I shout. "There's a reason never to learn," he shouts back.

Is this terrible? I fleetingly wonder. Is it awful that my kids, both of them out of the house with jobs and lives of their own, don't actually know how to make a bed? It's because we don't use top sheets, never did, only the fitted kind on the bottom, and duvets on top—bed-making European-style, right? Bed-making made easy. However. I grew up in a house where the flat top sheet cuffed the blanket just so (was supposed to anyway); and at the bottom, the bed was wrapped like a present, with hospital corners.

And that's how my mother likes a bed. And my mother is coming, my mother's idea. Months ago, she called to propose we get tickets to hear something at Disney Hall. And I sensed right away how invested she was, and how wary—braced for me to balk—what if I said no, what if I came up with an excuse. As if I ever would. Still, for her to have to have a reason, an event in the bargain in order to visit her daughter on the other side of the country; to hear that edge of trepidation in her voice: at once, I felt sad and guilty. I should have done the inviting—she'd hinted around and I'd let it slide. Thinking she, too, would let it slide—thinking she didn't mean it, my mother, who doesn't much like LA; my mother, who is old and lonely and bewildered—older and lonelier (and bewildered-er) than she cares to admit; and, also hard to admit, we don't get along very well, she and I, not for more than a couple of days. But such a long trip to take for just a couple of days. So I shouldn't have been surprised when she suggested we make an exception to the guests-are-like-fish rule. Not a good idea, said I too quickly. You'll get bored, I said. You'll get antsy. You don't like Los Angeles, remember? Then her turn to remind me that travel takes a toll at her age. The time zones, she whimpered. And that's when I suggested she plan to go north to see my brother for the balance of the week. North to San Francisco, where she'll stay in a hotel, it's true. "Why can't she stay in a hotel in LA?" asks my daughter. Because, I say, she counts on staying here—because I'm the one she can stay with. The one who most upsets her, perhaps, but also the one she's known longer than just about anyone. We go way back, my mother and I, back before even the second husband (who raised me; for that, I am grateful—to *her*), and, now that most of her family and friends are dead, who knows her as I do, as long and as well? More to the point, who else wants to please her? Who cares as much what she thinks and whether she approves?[1] As if she ever would approve; as if, as she says, she's going to perform according to any script other than her own—as if I haven't learned that by now.

As keen as I am, as hopeful as I am (the elaborate preparation), I do know: by Sunday night I'll be biting my lip; and Mom? She'll be tunelessly humming as she does when she's vastly, or even only slightly annoyed.

However, she is coming. My mother is coming! The bed is a vision, you should see. There's a good loaf of sourdough in the breadbox, fruit in the bowl, full-fat cottage cheese in the fridge. And—this is especially important—heavy cream, unpasteurized, for her coffee, which is the reason for this whole convolution. It's coffee-inspired. That glass bottle

---

[1]This *is* a woman with a mother complex.

of cream—that should tell us something. Should tell *me* something, I mean. My mother will not be impressed with my coffee, not as I dream of her being—

Coffee just isn't her bag, her *thing*—cream is. The right kind of cream. A three-minute egg, buttered toast, good preserves (no pectin), fresh orange juice—but coffee? No. See here, the answers from her coffee questionnaire:

When did you start liking coffee?
I have always liked coffee. People tell me that I am not a real coffee lover because real coffee lovers drink it black. I hate black coffee.

But further down she writes: *I am very particular about coffee. I would rather have nothing than either lousy coffee or tea. I never have coffee on a plane. Except on European airlines I have never had a decent cup of airborne coffee.*[2]

And she adds:
I still love Chock Full o'Nuts, spiked for the last fifty or more years with 25 percent French Roast.

See, I know by now (I didn't always: I happily bought and drank it for decades myself, of course I did—because my mother . . . !), Chock Full o'Nuts isn't good. Chock is

---

[2]Nor should anyone else, on any flight to anywhere, not if we don't want to get sick: https://www.travelandleisure.com/airlines-airports/flight-attendants-dont-drink-coffee-tea-planes.

humdrum first wave coffee.[3] The stuff Americans (and the rest of the world) have been drinking for generations, the stuff in those vacuum-sealed cans at the grocery store—not the good stuff. Unless you think it is. Unless you love it. In which case, who's to say you shouldn't, or you don't—

Nobody gets to judge the other guy's coffee—coffee is personal. Coffee is particular.

And—there's another lesson here, Dinah, just for you: Say, tomorrow morning, your mother doesn't think very much of your (wonderful) coffee (much less like it); say she isn't impressed, say she doesn't notice that it's any more or less delicious than hers, the kind she makes at home—say she sniffs or shrugs, even frowns in disapproval, starts to hum when you tell her about the Trystero,[4] who delivers coffee on Wednesdays (*only in LA . . .*), a variety of beans from a variety of sources that he cooks in a tiny turquoise roaster (meaning it would take up only a counter, as opposed to the

---

[3]Referring all the way back to the 1800s, when big business saw coffee farms as a commercial opportunity. What had heretofore been an exotic beverage, became commonplace with the advent of pre-roasted, pre-ground beans. In cans. Available at your local grocery. By the 1920s, Hills Brothers had invented the vacuum seal; the Japanese had figured out how to freeze-dry the grounds for an *instant* cup; and then came Mr. Coffee, all the way from Germany. The emphasis was on ease, speed, affordability, that's what characterized the first wave.

[4]Greg Thomas is his name, and he has a thing for Pyncheon: not only the brand, but two of his regular weekly offerings get their names from *The Crying of Lot 49,* an early novella, in which coffee apparently plays a pretty minor role. If you're keen on coffee references, the one to read, says Greg, is *Mason & Dixon.*

whole kitchen) in a garage in Lincoln Heights. When you went there to meet him, to see what he does, how he does it, there was no place to sit. It was August! It was a hundred million degrees! And the Trystero has long, straight hair, silky fine—it grows way past his shoulders—and *he* had to stay there all day, roasting, sweating, whereas you were back in your car in under an hour. Frown she may, your mother, as if it were pretentious to have specialty coffee delivered to your door. But this guy is an artisan, right? An entrepreneur. He should be commended! For vision, imagination, customer service. He's trying to make a living, and he deserves every nickel, too. (All of you complaining about spending four or five dollars for cup of coffee, do you have any idea how much time, effort, experience went into the making?)

Hold on, though, I'm getting ahead of myself.

About my mother: she doesn't have to like my coffee. Although, just to say, if I'm too old to need her approval, she's too old to withhold it. (Oh Mom, what a pair we are, and what bunk we hand down from mother to child; now taking a vow, therefore, to always book a hotel room wherever they are, my own kids, wherever I'm visiting one or the other.)

Back to coffee, back to my poll, the one I sent around so many months ago, it began with a question about personal history and associations: *Like bread and eggs*, wrote my mother, *it was always just there*. Exactly. I could say just the same. Always there—bread, eggs, coffee. And Mom. She was always there, too.

THE QUESTIONNAIRE

Hello dear friends,

I happen to be writing this little book about coffee—
if it's not too much trouble, may I interview you, please? (You
can answer in monosyllables)—

Starting with your:

1. Coffee memories:

   - Were you aware of coffee as a kid?
   - Who drank it at your house?
   - Were you allowed to drink it?
   - When did you first try it? (If you ever did.)
   - When did you start liking it? (If you ever did.)

2. If you drink coffee now:

   - What kind? (Brand or whatever)
   - How do you make it? (Drip or whatever)
   - How do you drink it? (Black or white, cream or
     milk, sugar or . . . or no sugar)

3. If you've given up coffee, how come?

4. How often do you drink it? When? And why? (For the lift, for the taste, for the ritual?)

5. Do you like anything special with your coffee? (Cookies? Tobacco? Brandy? Bacon?)

6. Are your associations with coffee generally good/bad/indifferent? (Do they involve music, art, books, films, seasons, anything specific? Of all of those, what's the first thing that comes to mind?)

Also if you're up for it, which do you *generally* prefer:

Morning or evening?

Eating in or out?

The city or the country?

Classical or jazz?

Sweet or savory?

Cake or pie?

Cake or ice cream?

Muted or bold (colors, I mean)?

Lakes or oceans?

Woods (mountains) or deserts?

Heels or flats?

Spring or fall?

Drama or comedy?

Pop or jazz or classical or rock and roll?

Coffee or tea?

Coffee when you make it yourself, or when somebody
else does?

*

"Mom," says my son, when I ask him if he's ever going to respond, "you should use survey monkey. Nobody's going to take the time to fill out that thing."

Survey monkey—what is survey monkey? We bicker then—and this is generational, must be. If he isn't willing to deal with striping and pasting into an email, I'm certainly not about to click on a link to a survey, nothing doing, no way.

Meanwhile, 20ish out of 30ish people do bother to reply. Not my own children, it's true; and only a couple of millennials who were probably just being polite (so it is with former students, and the sons and daughters of friends in the neighborhood). That should give you an idea how scientific the enterprise.

3 COFFEE-MILK

Coffee is your ally.

—HONORÉ DE BALZAC

The little girl doesn't know what the lemon is for; or how the mother, the beautiful mother—pale skin, black hair, high bones,[1] sure fingers (see how they twist the peel just so)—can drink what looks like oily ink with a layer on top of yellow-brown goo,[2] though she does loves the tiny cup in its saucer—

And her mother, she loves her beautiful mother, the most beautiful grown-up in the world. She will grow up to be just like her (she can hardly wait): she'll have little china cups (and fish forks, and butter knives); and bath oil, and eyeliner, and sheer hose, and drippy earrings; and at dinner parties— all dressed up, with her hair in a twist—she'll decorate her tiny cup of coffee with a perfect yellow curl.

---

[1] Think Audrey Hepburn in *Breakfast at Tiffany's*.
[2] The crema on top of an espresso—also known as "the Guinness effect," and a function of the roasting and brewing of darker roasts.

(Sidebar: Most of this never happens. Although she does acquire butter knives. But never once in the ensuing five plus decades has she ordered a Caffè Romano (espresso, in English and Italian, with shaving of lemon).)

For now, the little girl occasionally drinks coffee-milk: a tall glass of skim with room for a half inch of coffee and a teaspoon of sugar, the only way she can get it down, which, she is told, she must do—otherwise she won't grow. But she only gets to have this delight every third or fourth day—if she drinks too much coffee, the mother explains, it will stunt her growth. (Stunt! Such a terrifying word.) Even so, she hates the milk all by itself (still true): when she isn't permitted just that little bit of coffee, what does she do? She waits her mother out—every morning the mother exits the kitchen, crossword puzzle in hand, to run a bath—then pours the whole glass down the sink. "Did you drink your milk?" calls her mother from the tub. She shouts back that she did. But not so—she has never had a full glass of milk in her life, not that she remembers, and look, she grew anyway. She thought she might never stop growing. It was awful to be so tall, except she did get to play the male leads at Waukeela Camp for Girls. And eventually, her mother got wise, stopped pushing the milk, let her have as much coffee as she pleased. Finally, at five feet eight inches (not so towering—though on family vacations her cousins called her Wilt, for Chamberlain, which was horrible) she was done. What she now knows? Those cousins, grown men on the short side, were jealous even then. Also, coffee doesn't stunt anything. File that one under coffee myths.

Whereas to be filed under truths, if not exactly facts, even espresso doesn't have to be bitter: it shouldn't need that lemon—or sugar, or milk—

However, subjectively speaking ("Everything that is worthwhile is to some extent subjective," said Nabokov)—if coffee makes milk less disgusting, milk (as disgusting as it is) makes most things more delicious. Especially coffee.

FROM THE COFFEE DIARIES #1

I'm thinking my grinder is swell, my cute little grinder with the single blade—my *inferior* grinder, said my mother the first time she saw it. "That gadget," she said, "is inferior. It cannot possibly achieve a consistent grind." What I think? As old as it is (I bought it a quarter century ago), it's amazing it works at all. In fact, it works very well! You want to know my method? I load the beans almost to the top, press my palm on the lid, and count. I count to ten fast three times, or until the sound sort of turns from a rumble to a whine, and then I stop. Then off with the lid, and that smell, I could swoon, I swear, but I do not wallow, I don't waste any time: right away, I scoop the grounds into the Chemex—three parts medium to one part French roast. Give or take. And then I start pouring. Three scoops means I'll take it just under the glass bubble on the side of the pot; four seems to call for half an inch or so more. It's a matter of feel, and the color of the drip, which starts out dark, and gets lighter, of course, but it mustn't get too pale. So you see how scientific this isn't—how wrong, how very wrong it must be, but I'm telling you I make the *most* delicious cup of coffee, everyone says so: *This is the best coffee*, they all say.

4 MY EMERGING PALATE

Who loves coffee more, you or dad?
I do. He does. He does, I do. I don't know—we both do!
But do you love coffee if you love it with milk and sugar?
Yes! You love it with milk and sugar.[1]

—FROM *THE COFFEE DIARIES*

Sitting upstairs on the stove is this morning's coffee, lukewarm, waiting for me to decide that I'm ready to drink it as is, or just a bit cooler once I add a little milk; see, I'm not above adding milk to my coffee, or drinking an afternoon glass at room temp. In fact (did you know? I did not), it turns out that one of the joys of an excellent cup of coffee is to savor the taste as it cools. What I always thought? The first sip

---

[1]Fred takes his coffee very light with two sugars. I use slightly less milk and no sweetener at all.

is the best; doesn't get better than this. It turns out if you're patient (don't gulp!), if you cultivate those taste buds—a cup of coffee will get better and better, different-er and different-er; the upshot being that the very best coffee really is "good to the last drop"—good! delicious!—but not the *same*. Says who, you ask. Say the experts—the aficionados of coffee—moreover, they warn about the effects of the microwave:[2] not that I'm above microwaving my coffee, god knows, although to change up its chemistry, profile, flavor, and that's what a microwave does, isn't the idea, not if it's flavor you're after, not if you appreciate flavor, unless (my gosh, this sentence, talk about caffeinated)—unless—well, maybe we like the difference, you and I. Or we *think* we do. Or maybe, subtle as it is, it doesn't register, quite, and we sure do like the temp. If that's so? If we don't mind our coffee slightly altered, or if we just don't notice—well, fine, okay, say those experts, those nerds, which is what they call them*selves*, by the way—*coffee nerds* (I'm not casting aspersions, not I). *However you like it*, they insist, *we wouldn't presume, we're not the "flavor police."* That's what they *say*.[3] But you know—I do, too: they wince when they catch us reheating; they politely look away when we add sugar or cream (unless we're drinking a very dark

---

[2]https://www.thedailymeal.com/drink/best-way-reheat-coffee; https://www.tastingtable.com/cook/national/reheat-coffee-microwave-leftover-lacolombe-Caribou; https://driftaway.coffee/temperature/.
[3]Jordan Michelman and Zachary Carlsen, *The New Rules of Coffee* (Ten Speed Press, 2018).

roast—which is only not-suspect, itself, if we're aware that the taste we're enjoying has not a lot to do with the properties of the original fruit).

And what if you were to opt for a vanilla or hazelnut latte? (I would *never*.) Don't think those well-meaning nerds (farmers, roasters, Q-graders,[4] baristas) wouldn't want to educate you: to explain that the good stuff is already sweet, complicatedly so. It already tastes of some combination of berries, or flowers, or spices, or citrus, or nuts, or tea, or tobacco (*tobacco!*), or varieties of chocolate; just *taste* it, they're dying to say, coffee tastes of so many things, depending on where it's from—the *terroir*[5]—and how it was processed (natural or washed—one way isn't cleaner than the other, just more controlled), and then roasted (to bring out the various notes, or to burn them away)—and if they catch us making a pot without weighing the beans (but at least we do grind them at home, except—are they fresh? Did we use the right kind of grinder?), without *exactly* gauging the temperature of the water; and, just speaking for myself, my pour-over skills are not perfect—my gosh, there are so many

---

[4]Certified coffee analysts: their skills (olfactory and otherwise), along with a common vocabulary, enable them to judge coffees from all over the world for their various properties and overall quality.

[5]A word originally associated with wine, most literally to do with the soil, but where coffee is concerned it refers to all the physical conditions and more: not only the soil and the climate, but the producers, their community, their expertise. https://www.perfectdailygrind.com/2018/03/what-is-terroir-and-why-does-it-matter/.

ways to get coffee wrong. And yet—it's pretty hard to get it wrong, am I right?[6] So (she shrugs, throws up her hands)—so: whatever else you *shouldn't* do to your coffee, *didn't* do to your coffee, the point is, if you want that leftover cup—if I do, anyway—well then, rules shmules! Coffee is personal, what did I say? Knock yourself out. Or, rather, go ahead: drink up and be restored. Thank you, I will.

The thing is, though, I should get to it soon. Before three p.m., say. But what if I'm not ready by then? Shouldn't it be my prerogative to push my treat till four, four-thirty, five?

Sidebar: Some people do drink coffee all day long—it's the river running through it. But for many of us others? Coffee is the dock in the bay, the point of departure and return—the moment before, anticipated, extended, improvised, framed, casual or formal, serious or serendipitous . . . (Sorry, I digress all over again. But this, too, is part of the story, how coffee encourages not only focus and industry, but reverie, reflection, rambling, parentheticals . . .)

Re this afternoon—re so many afternoons when I'm lagging and dragging or even feeling actually productive and inclined therefore to treat myself—to know there's a bit of old coffee on the stove, to know I will forget-then-remember it's there, and run up to drink it, not hot, not cold, not

---

[6]Although once you have learned how to do it right, once you know how coffee can taste, what it can be, it's hard to get it down the old (wrong) way.

because I'm falling asleep, but just for the *taste* of it—see, this is new. Today's brew, by the way, is a blend, with notes of milk chocolate, mandarin, and honeysuckle. So says the label. Someone (not I) was able to identify the exact kind of citrus and flower, dear god. I could only have told you it was different from yesterday's. (A single origin from Peru—oh listen to her; listen to me, will you?). That said, I do seem to have become a person who actually *tastes* her coffee! Who knows when it's good. Who wouldn't drink it if it weren't. (Except in diners, I love diner coffee, which is often excellent, but even when it isn't, I love how the waiters keep filling and filling my cup.)

So two questions: first, when did this happen to me? And second, a less thrilling development, when did I get so old that I need to factor in how much I've already sucked down and when, as in what time of day. An affront, this is, this sort of calculation: you want to know why? Ask almost anyone, coffee is for grown-ups.[7] To be *so* grown-up, so *old,* that I can't just drink it whenever I like? Because I'm worried about sleeping through the night? That just isn't fair.

---

[7]As confirmed in the bulk of those returned questionnaires. See #1: *Were you aware of coffee as a kid? Who drank it at your house?* Mothers and/or fathers, that's the answer every time. "It was a talisman of adulthood," wrote one friend. And another remembers asking for sips, and then "making faces and retching sounds."

However. Back to question number one, an emerging palate at my advanced age: why, how? And that's easy—that's a recent development tied to my research, however informal. I only had to start to notice, that's all, there's a novel idea, and an angle worth pursuing besides: coffee as a metaphor for all the things a person takes for granted. On a daily basis. For the ways in which a she puts her head down, allows life to simply happen, if not exactly pass her by. To wit, for years we drank Chock Full o'Nuts at our house, because that's what our parents drank, not just mine, Fred's, too. That alone, we figured, was a sign of some sort, as if A., we needed a sign; and, B., hundreds of thousands of people didn't also drink Chock. Chock was a chain, like Schraffts, like HoJo's and the International Pancake House. (Way back when, we'd hang out after school at the New Rochelle Chock Full o'Nuts, though we never ordered coffee—blech, coffee was for grown-ups—only Cokes and fries.)

But the counters pretty much disappeared in the 70s[8]. Only the coffee, so named for their signature sandwich (cream cheese and chopped nuts on raisin bread—no nuts in the grounds themselves, of course not), remains. In varieties, by the way, including Soho Morning, Midtown Manhattan, and Upper West Side Dark Roast; and even so, even as we pined in those years for New York (as if coffee could bring it closer, but if anything could . . .), eventually, sometime in the 90s, we got bored; or I did, anyway. Playing house in SoCal—

---

[8]A store opened on West 23rd Street in the aughts and closed again two years later.

that is married with children and dogs and a faltering career (as an actor), and looking to spice up my pantry (another metaphor)—I'd loiter in the coffee aisle at Gelson's,[9] picking brands willy-nilly, for the names (Lavazza), or the slightly more elegant cans (Illy), or the colors (Café Bustelo). Even after I discovered the second wave of coffee (and the third),[10] I was glad enough to buy a bag of grounds—never whole beans, hell no; given the choice, who would ever grind her own?—only once in a while. The cans themselves were so useful. Where better to store chicken fat, tea bags, hardware, paper clips, tiny tubes of tempera, assorted buttons, marbles, jacks, pencils, and pens—paintbrushes, of course. Think how

---

[9]Which was the Mayfair back then, before Trader Joe's moved in across the street, with their own bargain offerings, Bay Blend, Smooth and Mellow, Organic Bolivian, and that was when I first realized I could grind the beans right there in the store. But never mind the coffee—it was the gorgeous can-shaped containers (but made of cardboard, not metal or plastic). Remember Benetton? The sweaters stacked in shades from light to dark? I remember wanting them all, not to wear, but to have on display. Same deal with Trader Joe's coffee, ha.

[10]More about waves: if the first sacrificed quality to commerce, the second, starting with Peet's (founded in Berkeley, California, in 1966), followed by Starbucks, answered the consumer's desire for better, changed up our vocabulary to accommodate espresso concoctions, and turned coffee-drinking into a cultural, socially-defining experience, leading to the third wave, focused on artisanal production, reminding us of the farms and farmers whose existence makes our triple, venti, nonfat, half-sweet macchiato possible. But that's not all—there's a fourth wave, too, doubling down on social consciousness and science, and determined to source only the highest quality beans; and a fifth! How is the fifth different? It appears to assume high quality, turning our attention to the business of coffee, the professional opportunities across the board for a new generation.

Jasper Johns immortalized Savarin, which, unlike good old Chock, is otherwise available no more.

When did we leave off those cans altogether? I don't remember. Gradually, I'd say. To the point, though: however much I've recently learned about coffee, including how exquisitely nuanced a flavor it is, how astounding to think of all those decades of drinking (enjoying, depending on, loving) not-so-great brands, two, three cups a day, which is proof, I'd say, wouldn't you?—my emerging palate aside, coffee is about so much more than coffee.

As to the answer to question number two: when did I get so old. Decades, I said, didn't I? Decades have passed, that's how.

And I should be honest: though by now I grind the beans fresh every morning (almost); and, by now, I wouldn't dream of committing to any one brand (how did I think that sort of narrow-minded fealty was the pinnacle of adult sophistication?); though I'm curious these days about the beans I haven't tasted or tried, what I crave first thing still, is the heat, the jolt. When the coffee is especially rich or fragrant or fruity, hooray. But the reason for that very first cup? The *grounding*, not the grind. To get a grip on the day. If ever there were a symbol of here and now, it's coffee; standing in for every coffee that came before, preparing a person to get on with whatever comes next; holding her in between, suspending the present, whenever it is. Coffee lets us start, and start again, and start over—however old a person feels, however stunned to have gotten so old, fortified with coffee, she can carry on.

A COFFEE STORY (THIRD-HAND)

A couple are invited to dinner at the neighbors (says my friend who's acquainted with the couple), who turn out to be coffee people. Their host has a job in the industry, travels the world in search of beans, smelling, tasting, sipping, slurping, or whatever it's called (cupping![1] That's it!)—he knows his trade, talks coffee all through dinner, and afterwards prepares a pot just for them, which takes him a long, long time; they wait and they wait, until finally, he returns to the table with a glass carafe and four little cups. He carefully pours. "Just taste," he tells his guests, when he sees them scanning the table for sugar and cream. "You'll see, no need to add anything at all." But, they confide to my friend and theirs the next day, the coffee is terrible. Weak. Pale. The weakest, palest coffee in the world, weaker than the worst

---

[1] The procedure by which the professionals assess the merits of the bean. Small samples are roasted and separately ground, smelled dry, smelled wet, eventually slurped, and scored every inch of the way.

diner coffee, that's what they say. The caveat being, they're the first to admit, accustomed as they are to regular old coffee (which by now means Peet's, Starbucks, Intelligentsia, Blue Bottle), perhaps they'd need to educate themselves before they'd be able to taste how exceptional—

I guess that might be true. Except c'mon, they drink pretty good coffee, right? Long ago I moderated a panel with the late, great food writer, Jonathan Gold. He was there to discuss his craft with similarly established critics (cinema, rock and roll, books), all of whom had the opportunity to emphasize the value of introducing audiences to foreign and unfamiliar work. When I tried to let Jonathan off that particular hook, he protested: "Food can be difficult, too," he said. Food, maybe. But can and should coffee veer toward esoteric? Is there any pride to be had in appreciating a challenging[2] cup of coffee? As with experimental theater, for instance? Which, if I'm honest (former actor that I am), always seemed more interesting for the people on the stage than in the house. To know too much about anything can spoil it for you (and you for it), whatever it is. Like, I once dated a lighting designer.

---

[2]As opposed to bad—because to get down a bad cup of coffee, bad as in bitter, bad as in strong, that does positively signify, doesn't it? "That'll put hair on your chest," my dad used to say. Hair on our chests as an indication that we were not just stoic to have swallowed our medicine, but better for having done so. Fortified. Toughened up. (He wasn't anti-feminist; only a man of his own generation.) In other words, a bad cup of coffee isn't bad. On the other hand, a weak cup of coffee? There's just no reason in the world . . .

He took me to BAM (the Brooklyn Academy of Music) to see a show, I don't remember what, and neither would he, since he spent the whole hour craning his neck, looking into the rafters, counting the scoops, the spots, the reflectors. Better to know nothing and enjoy the show, the wine, the cheese, the mystery condiments and spices, no? I'm asking, re coffee: is there virtue in working at liking it? Shouldn't it just taste wonderful? And isn't wonderful a matter of taste?

Meanwhile, I recently met a coffee person, a bona fide expert, Teresa von Fuchs[3]—if anyone knows about coffee, it's Teresa, and she says ask people about coffee, people who drink coffee every single day—and who talks about the *taste*? Nobody, that's who.

---

[3]See Chapter 5.

5 WHAT WE TALK ABOUT WHEN WE TALK ABOUT COFFEE (TERESA WAS RIGHT)

It's at the end of my interview with a friend whose dad was an executive at Maxwell House Coffee that we get to the gold. Not that I'm not interested from the start: Tom's father's first job out of high school was in the mail room at the original plant in Hoboken, New Jersey. And, it's true, he says, the whole town smelled of coffee. Hoboken? Really? Now, writing this, I wonder (I forgot to ask): was that stimulating? Intoxicating? Did the coffee aroma overwhelm other smells, good and bad?

In any case, except to go to war, Tom's dad never left the company. Once back in the States, he studied chemistry on the GI bill (first put into law in 1944, to fund programs for returning veterans). He was even on the team that first freeze-dried the grounds. Some years into his tenure, he was named Manager of Quality Control, and in one of his last projects—with the aim of debunking various myths—he organized a study of previous studies related to coffee and health. For example, Tom asks, do I realize coffee is *not* a diuretic?[1] People think it is, but, no, coffee doesn't make you pee; only, if you already have to go, it will increase the sense of urgency. When I make a face in confusion, he clarifies: You don't pee more or faster on coffee, even if it feels like you do. And it will. That's a physical fact of drinking coffee, that feeling, that need.

By this time we've been talking for nearly an hour—I should let the guy go. Instead, for some reason, I press one last time, about his associations, good, bad, indifferent (besides his father); and what "pops into my head," Tom says—

"I'm going to teach in Copenhagen—"

"You are?" I interrupt.

"No, no, this was years ago," he says. But he's suddenly in present tense, that's the thing; it's the 90s—1992 to be exact—two weeks before he has to be in Denmark, and he flies to Paris, meets a friend, rents a car, and together they drive down to Morocco—do I know those beautiful dunes in the Algerian desert? I nod, even though I don't. (Because I want him to keep talking, this story he's telling, so evocative, so *cinematic*—) In Algeciras they board the Ferry to Tangiers,

---

[1] There does seem to be some debate about this. According to the Mayo clinic, while coffee can count toward our daily fluid intake, and does not cause dehydration, "caffeinated drinks may have a mild diuretic effect."

and on deck they down shot after shot of espresso and brandy. What time of day? I ask. Didn't matter, he says. Was it great? I ask. He says it was. "I don't know why the brandy, it was just what people drank on the boat," he adds, almost to himself, focused somewhere over my shoulder now, as if looking out to sea.

6 COFFEE IN BROOKLYN

So ask people about the best cup of coffee they ever had, they'll tell about a place—a city, a town, a beach, a bay, the swim or hike or happening that occurred just before or after that great cup of coffee, or even *during*. Like, once, on a family trip in the Berkshires, some of us were walking through the woods, not more than a mile from the house, when one of my cousins, just out of the Israeli army, stopped like the soldier he was to build a tiny fire, pulled a miniature tin pot, dented and scarred, from his knapsack, and brewed us each a little cup of coffee right there on the path. Who remembers how it tasted? Even at the time, who cared? We were only charmed. Ask about a good cup of coffee, you'll hear about the maker, the cups or mugs (or even the double-wall glasses), the room, the table, the view, the trees, the sand, the color of the sky—the weather! Weather very often figures into coffee stories,[1] as does time of day, time of year,

---

[1] Check out social media for the following popular hashtags (to name just a few): coffeeintherain, coffeeinthesun, coffeeinthesnow, coffeeatthebeach,

time of life—and so the partner, the spouse, the parent, the friend old or new—

Right you were, Teresa. Right you were, right you are. From now on, by the way, when I'm asked about coffee, I'm bound to remember having coffee with you. With Teresa von Fuchs, VP in charge of sales with Bellwether Coffee.[2]

And what is Bellwether? Why is it notable? Well—at Bellwether, they've developed this groundbreaking new roaster. I've seen it, too, at their headquarters up in Berkeley, on Co-Ro[3]—except Ro isn't short for "row," so "at" would be better. *At* Co-Ro, a collaborative roasting facility where Bellwether shares space, storage, equipment with something like twenty-five different companies. Although it's not the community roasters that Bellwether's using, it's their own. Not beautiful in the old way, not massive and shiny—no visible pans, drums, and funnels—none of that curling up to the ceiling, no venting through the roof up into the sky: how did Bellwether manage to contain all of that? They just did.[4] Thanks to their designers, those polluting old geezers (however recently manufactured and installed) are a species possibly endangered. On their way out if the Bellwether roaster catches on. Which it should,

---

inthewoods, inthecity, andthecity, andrain, andsun, andclouds—and, of course, a whole other thing, but how to leave it out? #cloudsinmycoffee! (More on that later.)

[2]https://www.bellwethercoffee.com/.

[3]https://www.corocoffee.com/.

[4]https://www.bellwethercoffee.com/roaster-details/.

which it must—which, if this year's Coffee Expo in Boston is any indication, it will: in competition with well-established brands, the Bellwether roaster won Best New Product, how not? It's the size of a fridge—streamlined, compact—and emission-free!

The downside, if there is one? None of those heady fumes or audio cues—the master roasters don't get to hear the first crack, or the second,[5] which have heretofore helped to define them as the masters they are, *but* you can still watch the happening through a glass window; and, anyway, those gases, in spite of the venting (because of it, too), aren't healthy for us or the world. Instead, the Bellwether roaster is programmed with "intuitive" software that not only controls all features of the process, but also allows sellers to choose from a curated list of producers and profiles, even to create their own, thus promoting transparency and fair compensation for all.

Whew. Where was I? Having coffee with Teresa in Brooklyn, that's where. We first met in a tiny shop—place, store, café—what do we call them now? Not restaurants, though they serve everything from croissants to kimchi to vegan pastrami, depending. At this one I ordered a bagel—I was starving, sweating, overdressed, it was raining—but never mind all that. A mutual friend had put me in touch

---

[5] Listen to them here: https://www.sweetmarias.com/soundsoffirstandsecond crack.php.

with Teresa. "She's a Q grader,"[6] said my friend, which went over my head at the time. A good thing, too, I was already flustered, already worried I'd embarrass myself—what did I know about coffee? Even less than I thought. But enough to be vaguely relieved when Teresa ordered first, a latte, which meant I could have one too.

After we sat down and started to talk, I got comfortable enough to ask about that. By then I'd learned that she takes her coffee black at home. "But it's ok," I asked, nodding toward our drinks, "to have it this way now and then?"

She laughed. As if I needed her permission. Then: "Most people don't love coffee," she said. "What they love is milk." Of course. Right again. When somebody *does* wax on about the *taste* of the best cup ever, seldom as that happens, it invariably involves at least a dollop of foam or cream.

Meanwhile, such a good time I was having, talking to Teresa about coffee, and milk, and assorted other things, I'd forgotten to write anything down. Near the end of our conversation, I opened my notebook: "So what else would you like people to know?" I asked.

---

[6]More about the Q-grader system: it quantifies a whole range of characteristics—acidity, body, flavor, finish, etc., etc., etc.—in order to objectively assess their quality. The Q graders have to take a course to learn how to consistently identify these various elements in coffee—to memorize thirty-six different smells, for instance. When they're ready they're tested with an exam in twenty-two parts to be completed within three days.

Coffee comes from "super far away," she said. And "every step of the process matters."[7]

If we only realized: coffee, personal trigger that it is, connects us with people we'll probably never meet. If we thought about that, couldn't it change our attitudes not just toward coffee but toward other human beings? And if we realized the implications, commercial, cultural, environmental, having to do with this most basic and familiar product, this beverage we absolutely take for granted—

If we understood the risks, the hazards, the financials, the stakes—we might be more attentive, respectful, tolerant, generous, grateful, less stuck in our navels—

Coffee. I had no idea, I really didn't, when I got into this. But I guess if we understood about coffee, we might have a chance. As a species. A sign of civilization, coffee might civilize us yet.

"Anything else?" I asked Teresa.

"It's picked by hand," she said. "It's the most beautiful example of how everything in our lives that we touch and hold and eat and wear and sleep on and need is made by people-even when it's made by machines, people program the machines and pack the boxes or dream up the ideas."

She raised her latte as if making a toast. "How many hands have touched this coffee, do you think?" she said.

She closed her eyes and sipped.

---

[7]There are ten steps from seed to cup: planting, harvesting, processing, drying, milling, exporting, tasting, roasting, grinding, and brewing.

7 TWENTY-TWO HANDS . . .

. . . that's how many: that's the number of people who might have touched your average cup of coffee, says Jay. Jay Ruskey, that is, co-founder (with Kristen, his wife) of Good Land Organics and Frinj Coffee, located not even two hours north of LA. They're actually growing coffee up there (so close!), just west of Santa Barbara, in an orchard with a view of the Pacific, vast and glinting below. Eleven people work for Jay full time, not including the pickers, of course, whom he hires according to the season, when the cherries are ripe. But assuming your coffee comes from Mexico, or Guatemala, or Columbia, or Brazil, or Ethiopia, or Vietnam—or any country in the coffee belt[1]—twenty-ish strangers have done their part.

And "yet," writes Dave Eggers, in *The Monk of Mokha* (about coffee entrepreneur Mokhtar Alkhanshali), much

---

[1] The area between the 23rd North and 25th South Parallel, including countries in Central and South America, Africa, the Arabian Peninsula, and Indonesia.

of which is staged in Yemen,[2] "these cups only cost two or three dollars. Even a four-dollar cup was miraculous, given how many people were involved, and how much individual human attention and expertise was lavished on the beans dissolved in that four-dollar cup." At that price, he goes on, "chances were some person—or many people, or hundreds of people—along the line were being taken, underpaid, exploited."[3]

The Eggers book, not yet opened, was sitting on my night table, when we drove up the 101 to meet Jay and see the farm. "Freddy, take pictures, please," you can hear me say at the start of the "tape" (unconvinced as I was that I and my iPhone could actually do two things at once—record and photograph—that I, not the phone so much, wouldn't screw it up somehow). I wanted photos of everything: the barn, outside and in; the collection of coffee pots—tin, stainless steel, glass, single cup, double boiler, and so on—arranged in a parade on a long tall shelf; the wide racks of beans (seeds), yellow-green, spread out to dry in the sun;[4] the trees in the orchard, and their blossoms, fragrant as jasmine (though how to get a picture of that)—and the cherries, themselves, in clusters, mostly red but some yellow ones, too.

But our tour began inside. With coffee—Frinj coffee, of course. First Jay ground the beans and boiled the water; then

---

[2] Arguably the birthplace of coffee.
[3] *The Monk of Mokha*, p. 90.
[4] Natural as opposed to washed process.

he poured slowly and continuously into the filter, enough for three little ceramic cups. I wanted to know if they were his favorites to drink from. He shrugged, as if to say coffee is coffee. It's the coffee that matters. And the coffee was excellent. Strong, but not bitter. How relieved I was that Fred didn't ask for milk and sugar. Not that Jay would have been insulted—or would he. Later, when I got up the nerve to ask if he always drinks it black, he admitted that he'll order a cappuccino in town every once in a while. But, he said, "I can't bring myself to put milk in my own coffee that I grew . . . I just can't do it." (Whew, I thought.)

After coffee, he took us out around the back of the barn, past a pond full of koi kissing the surface, looking for snacks (he threw them a handful of fish food), and onto a path that wound down and down, the orchard growing up on either side.

There are a couple of thousand coffee trees, Jay told us; twelve different varieties planted between the avocados overhead, poppies growing up in between, and passion-fruit blooms, Disney-esque, the flowers-from-another-planet, that's how I think of them. Also abundant—cherimoya, dragon fruits, two kinds of limes. We tasted both—and the coffee cherries—and I wondered out loud why we don't eat the fruit, sweet as it is. Because the tropics are unsanitary, Jay said. True or not, it still wouldn't make sense: two seeds per cherry (not a single pit like a Bing), not small (as with grapes), therefore not enough flesh to make snacking worthwhile. Although, to remove those two seeds, to clean them and dry them and sort them and roast them (and so on)—that's not labor intensive? It is. Mind-bogglingly so. And me already high (mind-boggled) with the colors, the fragrance (not a bit like coffee), the bees and the blossoms everywhere—and when we climbed back up the hill, there was that view: the blue-blue ocean blurring into a blue-blue sky.

Afterward, back in the barn, Jay pointed to a chart on the wall—Good Land Organics illustrated *Life Cycle of Coffee*—whimsical pen and ink drawings of phases of pre- and post harvest, the plants, the machines, and the penultimate image, a pair of hands sorting the beans. Finally, the bag—a package labeled *California Coffee, Grown, Processed and Roasted at Goodland Organics,* stamped with their logo, a fruit-bearing tree.

We sat down at the counter again, and Jay explained about his plans. He'd been a small farmer for twenty-eight years, he said, but not anymore, his ambition to expand literally fueled by fire. Not so long ago the Ruskeys nearly lost the family farm. These days their forty-two acres is the Frinj flagship entity; but now they're involved with forty-seven coffee farms from Santa Barbara down to San Diego counties. The Frinj website promises that coffee offers California farmers a way "to diversify their farm portfolios." "And one way to subvert colonialism," says Jay, "is to grow the stuff here."

Subverting colonialism: Jay knows as well as anyone—that's what the third and fourth waves are all about; a way of making reparations as well as profit; of giving back as much as we take. And that's great, says Jay, he's all for it. But anywhere you can grow an avocado, you can grow a coffee tree. So why not in California? Never mind about all the things that can go wrong with any crop, for any number of people or fruits in the chain. Front and center on the website, Jay Ruskey announces his mission: **Our goal is to make Southern California the next specialty capital of the world.**[5]

Might this even be a way to save coffee? Because coffee is in trouble—not only because nobody's making enough money, not only due to poverty and political conflict in the places where it's still mostly grown, but because of climate change. Which, as noted, Jay knows firsthand. It's not like he lives in a decimated village in the war-torn Middle East, no. Still, this privileged son of upper middle-class Angelenos, whose family has been able to educate and support him, has paid his dues. His suffering in the wake of the California fires was real (he was evacuated from his property for nine days) as is his resolve to make this coffee-thing work, for himself, and for the rest of us. Real and admirable, too.

With all this on his mind, Jay is consciously raising and educating farmers, a daughter and two sons. Whatever they wind up doing with their lives, even if they don't take over the business, they'll know more than most of the trials and rewards that come with working the land. And not just in Goleta, California. When we met, Jay was reading *The Monk of Mokha* with his daughter, age eleven, who, he boasted (in his understated way), was already developing a discerning

---

[5]https://frinjcoffee.com/.

sense of smell and taste. Had I read the book yet, he wanted to know. Mokhtar, the hero (then on book tour with the author), is a friend, he said. (Later, when I finished the Eggers, I decided Jay and Mokhtar must have met through a Blue Bottle connection. Both men are in business with the Oakland-based company.) There's much to be proud about, and Jay is quietly but palpably proud.

But does he love coffee? The drink itself? Though I asked more than once, bent as I was (am) on that emotional, personal connection, I couldn't get him to enthuse. He drinks it—he likes it, certainly—but Jay isn't one to kvell. You can't "not think about the presentation and ritual," he said at one point, in response to my prodding, "but"—evidently wanting to talk about the farm more than anything else—"I'm more of a problem solver."

He just wasn't about to indulge nosy, sentimental old me—he had work to do: Limes, passion fruit, cherimoya, and cherries to grow, and pick, and process, and roast, and sell. He'd been generous to give me an hour—and anyway, how to separate his feelings about coffee from his livelihood; his devotion to his future, his family, his farm? Why would he? Why would I? What more personal connection could there be? About the brew itself—*his* brew anyway? When we ooh-ed and ahh-ed—*delicious! Isn't this delicious?*—for an anti-gush kind of guy, he seemed pleased.

A COFFEE STORY (FIRST-HAND)

"Well," says my old friend Sarah, "you should talk to Robert. Robert knows about coffee."

"Do you?" I ask. Robert is right there, at the kitchen island, sitting on a stool next to Sarah, his wife.

He sighs. "I would *like* to. I would like to be a coffee snob. But I don't actually know enough."

"Me too!" I say. "That's just how I feel: I would like to be a snob, but I know nothing!" (Self-disclosing,[1] this is true across the board, pretty much. I would like to be snob; I even am a snob; or no, not a snob, not really—and not a phony either. I'm just—I'm an enthusiast, that's what I am.)

I ask Sarah and Robert how they make their morning coffee. And they explain that when they were married, an old college friend (a woman I also used to know a little bit) gave them a lifetime supply. Of coffee. How generous, right? But

---

[1]This, I'm told, is a medical term, useful in psychotherapy. Not that I'm a therapist—I just like the way it sounds.

how is that done, that's what I want to know. And the answer: Nescafé,[2] that's how. They were given a Nescafé machine. It takes Nescafé capsules. Coffee pods. When they run out of pods they're supposed to let their benefactress know. Which Sarah couldn't possibly do, of course not, she can't bring herself to make that call—*Hello, how are you, time to send us more coffee*—but, objects Robert, it's supposed to be a lifetime supply. We're supposed to let her know—

So he did, and he did, and he did—

And then, finally, he suggested that the "giver" just go ahead and give up her Nescafé password. (At the kitchen island, Sarah rolls her eyes.) That way, he told her, he could order the coffee by himself, without bothering her, without taking up her time. (I look at Sarah. She looks resigned.)

"And you like it," I say. "The coffee, I mean."

"It's great," he says. "You can have all kinds of flavors."

"What about the environmental impact," I ask.

"They recycle," says Sarah. (Brightly. Hopefully.) "You return the pods and they use them again!"

"They *say* they do," says Robert.

---

[2] I know, I know, not Nescafé. I'm mortified, I am. What happened is I sent these pages to Sarah, fingers crossed she and Robert wouldn't mind my having fun at their expense. Ever-gracious, she wrote back right away: "Well observed and well remembered," she said, only "just one thing: it's a Nespresso machine. I think Nescafé is that yucky instant stuff. No one could be a coffee snob with Nescafé. ;-)." Busted, ouch.

RULES SHMULES (JUST A FEW, IN NO PARTICULAR ORDER)

1. Grind your coffee within ten days (two weeks at most) of the roast date on the side of the bag. (But if you happen to run out, only to stumble on some leftover beans in the back of drawer that you didn't know were there, well count yourself lucky. They'll probably make an excellent cup. So there.)

2. Don't buy coffee with a *sell-by* date. (As opposed to *roasted on*.) It probably isn't fresh. (But if you do, it's generally good within a year of the purchase, maybe longer. So there.)

3. Brew within fifteen minutes of grinding. (But like this morning, for instance, we used yesterday's grounds. And the coffee was marvelous, ha.)

4. If you're boiling water for coffee in an old-fashioned kettle don't begin pouring the minute it boils—take it off

the flame and count to thirty, or you'll scald the grounds.[1] (But if somebody else, like your beloved, gets to it first? And doesn't bother to count? Well, don't be so critical—choose your battles, honestly, when will you learn, you?—the coffee will be fine.)

5. Once brewed, drink it up right away. (Or whenever you want, see Chapter Two, about the joys of old, cold coffee.)

6. Really, though—this is a real rule, a rule that makes sense: don't put coffee beans, whole or ground, in the fridge. You may *freeze* them, once, in an airtight container (allow them to fully defrost before you grind). But to keep them in the fridge—it's a shanda—terrible to think how many people you know who store coffee there. All kinds of people. Last summer, in Paris, a helpful but misguided barista told me—in English and French, slowly, deliberately, lest I should misunderstand—to refrigerate my just-purchased bag of beans. I'd have argued, but for my pathetic vocabulary. (Que veut dire *too much moisture*? *Too much condensation*! Trop de *terrible advice*?) And may I just say: She was *French*! Therefore, we'd expect

---

[1] The best temperature for making coffee falls somewhere between 195 and 205 degrees. And water boils at 212. At sea level. (If you live in Boulder, Colorado, where it boils at 202: you can pour straightaway. The higher the elevation the lower the boiling temp.) Then, too, there's the size of the kettle to consider—and the material—those variables can also effect how long the water takes to cool a little. So it isn't crazy to invest in a thermometer. But I haven't. Not yet.

her to know better, would we not? Mon dieu, of all people, the French should know better! Just as, for instance, they know not to refrigerate eggs. Which are consequently so much tastier in France; but if American eggs lose something to effects of refrigeration, eggs at least are at encased and protected from its more egregious effects. Whereas coffee, whole bean or ground, is porous, impressionable, sensitive to light, heat, moisture, the elements. At the very least, the fridge will rob your coffee of its pungency (as with eggs—as with tomatoes, by the way, you know this, right? Don't ever put tomatoes in the fridge!)—at worst it will wind up tasting like steamed dumplings and chicken fried rice.

THESE THINGS ABOUT COFFEE ARE TRUE

1. It grows on trees. (It really does, though. As opposed to in cans in the grocery store. Or at Whole Foods, in barrels, in bulk.)

2. It was discovered in Ethiopia or Yemen some five or ten centuries ago, depending who you ask—

The Ethiopian story: Kaldi, the goatherd, circa AD 850, noticed his goats were especially lively after eating some berries, and tried them himself, and, in a whoosh of excitement brought them to a monk, who immediately realized how dangerous they were, and threw them in the fire, creating a fragrance so intoxicating as to cause them (Kaldi and the monk) to rush to recover the roasted beans and mix them with water—and presto: coffee! (Chances are this process has been abbreviated somewhat for the sake of the story, and it actually took a century or two to unfold . . .)

The Yemeni versions are various and similar, but they credit a bird, not goats, for discovering the fruit. Mokhtar Alkhanshali[1] has been quoted as saying that he believes the coffee cherry did first grow in Ethiopia, but found its way to Yemen, where the drink was invented by Sufis, and revered as a gift from God, to bring them to a higher consciousness— yada yada yada—the upshot being, if they can't take credit for the fruit, itself, the Yemenis were probably the first to cook it.

See, and that's no. 3, another true thing: coffee begins as a fruit! (And, repeating myself, the beans aren't beans at all; they're seeds.) Though coffee cherries grow in tighter clusters and are smaller than American Bings or Rainiers (or English Sunbursts, or French bigarreaus, or benishuhos from Japan). Less round, too, and heavier-skinned, two seeds per cherry,[2] encased in parchment, which has to be removed along with the mucilage. The trick, though, in spite of discarding the fruit, is to keep its particular properties in the final product; as with the relationship between grapes and wine (Concord, Pinot noir, Chardonnay), so it is with coffee cherries. Although I'd say those cherries—Gesha, Pacamara, Typica, Pink bourbon[3]—bear a less obvious relation to the end result.

---

[1] Dave Eggers's aforementioned book, *The Monk of Mokha*, tells the story of how Alkhanshali, against all odds, including civil war, not only became a coffee entrepreneur but also managed to put Yemen back on the coffee map.
[2] Though Fred found three in a single cherry in Goleta.
[3] All varieties of Arabica coffee.

When's the last time you ordered red or white coffee, right? And it's only the most discerning customer who wants to know if her espresso will have floral notes. But that's the goal of artisan producers—to pick and process those seeds (beans) without losing the qualities that distinguish one coffee plant from the next.

Speaking of which, here's another truth—no. 4: French roast is not a kind of coffee. Nor is it French, though it does refer back to the nineteenth-century way of roasting the beans till they're dark as can be. Ditto, espresso—*not* a kind of coffee. Not even a kind of roast! Instead the word refers to the preparation of the drink—shorter and more pressurized, forcing the water through an extra-fine grind as opposed to working with gravity (drip, drip), and resulting in a heavier, more concentrated brew. For espresso, the darker the beans the better. French roast, for instance, works well.

FROM THE COFFEE DIARIES #2

I've gone and bought a new grinder. Didn't snoop around much because the choice seemed clear: there was a brand recommended online, in stores, by my own little brother (mid-50s, pushing 6'3"), who is always my best resource—and he'd researched it for me (for himself, long ago, but this is how things are with us: he chooses the fixtures, the floor tiles, where to take our mother for dinner, and I gratefully, mostly, do as I'm told). So all I had to do was get myself to Crate & Barrel, where I bought it, the most expensive model they had (the best motor, said my brother). And I got it home, and I followed the directions (okay, I skimmed), and wound up with not even gravel. Pebbles, more like. I'd butchered my beautiful beans, lost half a pound of coffee, only to realize the machine wasn't properly put together, my bad. I took it apart and put it together again. Same deal, but worse, since this time—with what remained of the bag—I managed to spray coffee all over the kitchen. Like I don't have other things to do (read the directions for example); and this time when I tried to take the thing apart, the mechanism in question (the burr grinder: I know what that is *now*[1]) wouldn't budge. So. Many texts and photographs later (*Dinah,* said my brother, *if I lived down the street I'd come over*; Translation: Please stop torturing me)—back I went to Old Town, Pasadena. Where the store manager struggled with my grinder for a while, and then exchanged it for me. He even put the new one together while I watched. Was the first one a lemon? asked a friend. It was, I said. Or I turned it into one. (What to do with a lemon? Make lemonade. What to do with a coffee grinder? Make a lemon. Oh ha.) The thing is, once home, I had to dismantle it all over again, to clean it before first time use. Does it work? you ask. Stay tuned.

---

[1]It uses two cutting surfaces, not one, thereby chopping as opposed to slicing the beans.

8 SERIOUS BUSINESS

It's on Instagram that I find out about the Specialty Coffee Expo happening over the weekend in Boston. From a post, featuring the Chocolate Barista, by @sprudge, an online outlet for "global coffee culture and original journalism."

Coffee Expo 2019! How long this has been going on, I don't know (but the SCA—the Specialty Coffee Association—has been around for some thirty years): when I Google "how long has this been going on," up comes the Los Angeles Coffee Festival, happening in November 2019.

In LA, as with the Expo, there will be classes, competitions, awards ceremonies, seminars, workshops, parties; discussions and lectures about sustainability and the rain forest; luncheons, dinners, after parties; latte art; tastings, cuppings; coffee music, coffee art—which is not the same thing as that flower or heart etched in the foam of your morning fix. People actually paint with coffee: "The Starry Night" or the "Mocha Lisa,"[1] for starters, in shades of brown. (And originals, too; there's a board on Pinterest, "Art-Coffee Painting," featuring over 300 pins.)

---

[1] Created by American artist, Karen Eland: http://www.karenelandart.com/.

As for what I find when I click on the Chocolate Barista: a group formed to "[focus] on the promotion of racial diversity and inclusivity in the special coffee industry one black cup at a time." This year, at the Expo, they're having a party at Intelligentsia in Watertown (a Boston suburb) for people of color. There will be coffee, of course, and coffee-based cocktails, too.

And featured as this year's "Portrait Country," Burundi. That's funny. Just a few weeks ago I had no idea where to find Burundi on a map, shame on me. Now I know, it's south of Rwanda, west of Tanzania, and shares Lake Tanganyika (the longest freshwater lake in the world) with the Democratic Republic of the Congo to the west and Zambia to the south. It was because we were drinking coffee from Burundi—wonderful coffee[2]—that I got curious. Burundi is small and poor, but its government is apparently committed to expanding the production of specialty coffees, and to sustainable practices that will better the lives of farmers, sellers . . .

All of this is a roundabout way of insisting that coffee is confronting issues—sociological, cultural, commercial, political, environmental—all over the world. It's serious business and serious entertainment, to boot: there's such

---

[2]Fruity, chocolate-y, I'm wanting to say, and, when I check, the label reads "chocolate-covered cherries," which, though gratifying, doesn't mean I'd trust myself to articulate the difference between this one, and another from Burundi, both on the Trystero's weekly menu, described as tasting of tropical fruits, melon, and brown sugar—I'm just not that good—which is why I can't bear to bring my observations to the body of the text.

a thing as International Coffee Day, observed in twenty-five countries; and the following ten—China, Portugal, Denmark, Brazil, North Korea, Peru, Costa Rica, Ireland, Mongolia, Switzerland—devote another whole day of the year to national celebration.

And it's not just about one time or even annual events and festivities; there's even a Università del Caffè in Italy (main campus in Trieste, but there are twenty-five branches all over the world); thus far it's the only advanced degree program in coffee economics and science, but—at the Coffee Center at the University of California Davis, scientists, historians, and academics are developing another. Already they offer classes about coffee in continuing education, and for undergrads, too.

Take **Just Coffee**, for example, as described in the course catalogue like so:

> From its roots in Africa to its position as the world's favorite drink, the story of coffee is one rich in history and mythology. It is also a great lesson in biology and ecology, global climate change, development, trade and societal impacts. This course will help students understand the complex set of biological, ecological and social interactions that go into a truly "just" cup of coffee and how our food and agricultural systems interact with human well-being. Designed as a general education class suitable for students in all disciplines.

Sign me up.

9 SHOULDN'T COFFEE TASTE LIKE COFFEE?

It's the weekend. Where I want to be is in the hammock with a book: with Isak Dinesen on her coffee farm, or Honoré de Balzac in France, or just where a tree grows, in Brooklyn, where, as I remember, there is always a pot of coffee on the stove. Instead, I'm in downtown Los Angeles in the back room of a tony café—I've signed up for a Roastery Tour and Coffee Primer. There are six of us altogether, each having paid ten bucks to stand in circle and listen to this very young guy, who happens to be sitting. On a stool. And this is ass-backward, right? Not just that I'm old enough to be his mother: he's giving the lecture! He should be standing, we should be sitting—if only he'd offer me a seat (if he did, I'd demur)—but what was I thinking? A hot sunny Saturday afternoon, and I'm stuck in a windowless room lined with shelves stocked with bushels of beans, the roaster, itself, center stage, enormous and shiny, and complicatedly vented to send the fumes elsewhere, and what I wouldn't do for a whiff about now. Like smelling salts. To keep me going. But first, we have to learn the difference between varieties (Robusta and Arabica[1]); and about where coffee comes from, and good farming practices; and before we can taste anything, we have to watch our instructor, a soft-spoken, wispy-haired barista in a fisherman's cap with large plugs in both earlobes, choreograph not one but several perfect pour-overs . . .

At last, we get to sample his efforts, sipping from tiny paper cups, starting with the Sumatran.

"What do you taste?" he asks us one by one. What do I taste, what do I taste . . .

"Citrus?" he says hopefully. Citrus! Yes! Sure! Why not . . .

"Grapefruit?" Grapefruit. Huh. I guess.

"Honeydew melon and sweet pine?" he offers. I sip again. I ask for just a little bit more.

Then onto a blend from Africa. Again the instructor prompts us, "What do you taste?" Dark chocolate? says someone. Blueberry, says someone else. (By god, yes—I taste blueberry, too!) "How about fig?" suggests our guide. He visibly swishes the coffee around in the front of his mouth. Swallows. "How about lemon zest and golden raisin," he says. We're supposed to taste *raisin*? *Golden* raisin no less?

---

[1]Robusta is earthier, more caffeinated (stronger!), especially resilient, easier to grow, found mostly in eastern Africa and Indonesia—which explains Vietnamese coffee, cut with condensed milk and sugar, more dessert than beverage, but such are the demands of Robusta; whereas Arabica, sweeter, milder, more popular these days, doesn't need any milk at all.

Wait: shouldn't coffee taste like coffee? If coffee tastes like all these other things, what *does* taste like coffee? Why isn't anyone else confused?

The nice boy—he's only a boy—sends us home with a miniature bag of beans. I'm almost to my car when I realize I forgot to ask about the new grinder: how often do I have to clean it? It's worth going back, I decide. And, at first, I'm glad I did. The boy instructor is happy to reassure me: I don't have to clean the machine every day; more like every two weeks, he says. But can that be right? Does he know what he's talking about?

"Hey, when did you first fall in love with coffee?" I ask, before heading back out to the street.

"Honestly," he said, "between you and me? I'm more of a tea person."

(IF YOU SAY SO)

From Sigrid Nunez's *The Friend*:

> When I hear someone describe a wine as having a heavy
> black-pepper aroma followed by hints of raspberry and
> blackberry, I know they're full of shit. Show me the
> human that can smell a raspberry from a blackberry, even
> without having to go through pepper first.

So, A, okay, she's not talking about coffee, and B, she is
talking to her dog, marveling at his attributes, among
them his astonishingly sensitive nose. He could maybe tell
the difference between two kinds of berries, if he couldn't
describe it. People, she insists, aren't so gifted.

Nonetheless, re coffee, the following essences have been
identified (by people): dried berries/dried apricot/malt/
lavender/dark chocolate/chocolate-covered cherries [not to
be confused with] sweet black cherry/milk chocolate/stone
fruit/Baker's chocolate/ black currant/red apple/brown sugar

/raspberry/mandarin/honeysuckle/citrus/date/sangria/vanilla/hazelnut/orange/caramelized sugar.[1]

As well as these discrete flavor combinations: cranberry and fig; honey and orange; mandarin and honeysuckle; strawberry *and* jam [italics mine]; [not to be confused with] strawberry jam—

And getting even more specific, a coffee might be "limelike with buttery shortbread cookie"—or have a "grapefruit acidity [that] pairs perfectly with black tea complexity."

And certainly no less compelling are the following descriptions:

"exciting and easygoing"

"smooth, savoury, seductive" (from Canadian roasters, hence the flavorsome spelling)

[and as if it]

"prizes versatility."

Take that. Taste that. How does coffee do *that*?

---

[1]Brought to us by the following companies (in no particular order): Trystero Coffee, Groundworks Coffee, Sightglass Coffee, Stumptown Coffee, Verve Coffee . . .

10 COFFEE IN PARIS

A writer friend is planning a week-long workshop in France. She's bringing a chef, she says, and coffee from Portland. The woman across from her at the table (four of us are having dinner together), who has actually lived in France, who has a French husband, and speaks the language like a native herself, objects. A chef from Portland? Why? she asks. Why bring a chef to France? Because, says my friend, I can boss her around. But of course. Who's going to tell a French chef: no butter, no dairy, no gluten, no meat, no this, no that. Whereas. A chef from Portland. Okay. That makes sense. Also true, the second woman concedes, that French coffee is lousy.

French coffee is lousy? Really?

*

The French—they have these wonderful vending machines. For half a euro—one of those fifty cent coins, but it's not fifty cents, what is it? Fifty centimes? For fifty centimes, you can have a genuine espresso, no kidding. You hit the button and down plops a teeny, tiny plastic cup, and then out comes a shot in a syrupy stream, very dark, with just a dot of froth—a bubble, that's all—at the end. Or—for a euro, I think—you can have a café au lait; the paper cup, in that case, is just slightly larger. And I can't remember—is it simultaneous?—do the milk and the coffee descend at once, together, or first one then the other? In any case, the machine never gets it wrong. It's precise. It fills each cup just to the brim, never spills, never misses, never comes in short, very French, very civilized, no? Suspenseful, too. If you took your eyes away for even a moment you might miss something, that's what you think, that's how you feel. You're American. You suffer from FOMO. (So apt, that acronym, which I only just recently learned.)

Anyway. Vending machines notwithstanding, here's my theory: the French don't have to complicate their coffee. They have nothing to prove, nothing to feel better about (not on this score, politics aside): they're French! Whereas we Americans, if we're not insecure (it's tempting to suppose we are; that it's insecurity that accounts for our various pretensions), we do have a Fear Of Missing Out. Fear of missing anything! How to stay present under such circumstances? Meditation is one way, I'm told. And another? Specialty coffee. It's a destination, a place to sit down, a way to stop moving for a minute, and that is something the French know how to do. So, I'm saying, so what if their coffee is average at best? Not that they don't have plenty of venues for specialty coffee, if that's what you're looking for: but that's not what you want to be looking for, not in Paris, no way, the city is chockablock full of regular old cafés—that's what they're called in France. (I just realized: here in the states we have restaurants, diners, delis, wine bars, beer halls, tea shops, even—but the places that specialize in coffee? They're known by their proper names, right? Starbucks, Peets, Blue Bottle (Blue Bottle Café, OK, but who calls it that? Nobody), Groundworks, Intelligentsia, and other big chains, plus the independents just around here, say within three square miles? Thirty-odd places I can *name* for you off the top of my head.)

But in Paris. Café after café after café. But the café itself, the beverage, I mean, is beside the point. The point is to linger. To hang. To read, write, meet a friend, or just bask in the beauty and the life of the city. To pay attention—that's what French people know how to do. In a French café, if you start with an espresso or a crème (Order a latte? Get a crème; Order a cappuccino? Get a crème; A macchiato? Get a crème—you get the picture), chances are you'll stick around long enough to roll into a glass of wine. You might even wind up asking for the menu and ordering a bowl of moules, or a platter of steak tartare with a raw egg on top (when's the last time you saw that in your neighborhood?), though you won't feel obliged to eat or drink, not in Paris. Specialty coffee is our attempt to civilize ourselves, that's what I'm saying—the French are plenty civilized without it.

*

And now I'm thinking back to the first of five summers in Paris where I had a teaching gig—did we register that the coffee wasn't great? We did try a bunch of brands, I remember, summer after summer. We did, every single summer, buy a couple of one-cup Melittas in a housewares market on Rue Mouffetard—because we didn't like the Nespresso or the Keurig that invariably sat on the counter of each Airbnb, what was *that* about?

But out in the world, in all those cafés, did we notice the coffee was lousy? No. No way. Like the Americans we are, we ordered café au lait. Which, thinking back, taste-wise, wasn't anything special. And we didn't mind a bit. We even enjoyed it, savored it—didn't we keep having crème after crème? Because everything else was so wonderful: the light, the air, the trees, the flowers, the bread—my god, the bread—the omelets, the *salades*, the *glace vanille*—the action inside and out on the street—

Paris. A million places to drink coffee, everyone is drinking coffee everywhere. But they don't make a deal of it. There aren't forty-seven varieties to choose from. Or five different kinds of milk. And starting well before lunch, they're just as likely to be pouring rosé—or beer. Or *limonata*. They're not promoting a brand of anything—only a whole way of life, that's all. In Paris, you don't have to order up a cappuccino with soy, or whatever, to be the kind of person who takes time to be a person in the middle of the day. So the coffee mostly tastes the same from place to place, a bit better here, a bit worse there. It's just as Teresa told me (in Brooklyn): ask people about the best cup of coffee they ever had, they don't about talk about taste.

(One of) the best coffees I ever had: brought to you (to me) by Café Rostand in Paris, where we sat just behind a little old woman in a yellow cap, who was first delighted by the young foreigners at the adjacent table, and then, after they left, by an equally ancient gentleman whom she greeted with such effusiveness: "*Assaie-toi*," she said, patting the chair beside her, and gingerly they kissed each other's worn cheeks, spotted and crinkled, and she told him about the girls who had only just left (*les jeune filles adorables*) and then, minutes later, they rose together and ambled, shuffled, hobbled away, arm in arm, with their canes.

We finished our salades (niçoise for me, the house special for him, tiny crevettes in a mayonnaise dressing on a bed of butter lettuce—and, my god, the bread), and then we ordered two café crèmes, which came each with a cookie in the saucer and its own little pitcher of very hot milk. Across the street there was a clown entertaining the crowd walking in and out of the Luxembourg Gardens. We could have sat there all day.

A week or so later, during dinner with friends in a bistro not far from the Seine, I mentioned I was writing a book about coffee. "You should call it 'Carte Noire'!" said the woman sitting next to me. "Carte Noire? Really?" That's the coffee we buy (in Paris) when we realize we're all out of coffee, and it's late, and only the mini-mart on the corner is open, and that's all they have. (I don't say that to her. But Carte Noire—it's the supermarket brand, cheap, easy, ubiquitous—)

"It's regular old French coffee," she says, "and it's wonderful!"

Is it? We happen to have a bag at the flat. When we get there, I stick my nose in the grounds. Carte Noire. Smells bitter and stale. I'll drink it, but I won't like it, that's what I think.

The next morning, Fred's making his own little one-cup. We've got a bag from Coutume and another from Hexagone—both specialty shops on the right bank—but, wouldn't you know, the power of suggestion, he goes for Carte Noire.

How's your coffee? I ask.

Delicious, he says. Can we get this in LA?

In fact, I don't think we can—according to the site online it's available in France or the United Kingdom only (and how about this no-nonsense labeling: simply "rond et genereux" or "rond et équilibre"; none of that stuff about flowers and fruit—golden raisin, sweet pine—but what does it mean? How does "round" taste? And how is the flavor of "generosity" different from "balance"? And which would you choose? And anyway, it isn't very good, really not)—

But it isn't Carte Noire Fred wants back in Los Angeles: it's Paris. It's the view from the flat down Boulevard Gay Lussac, the quick jaunt from there to the Medici Fountain—the bread he'll bring back from the *boulangerie* on the corner—*une baguette traditionelle*—

It's Paris he's tasting, Paris he wants to take home.

11 EXTENDING THE METAPHOR

We're pretty much married to the Chemex[1] around here. Tried the French Press (the pot with a plunger, very popular), but the coffee gets cold too quickly, and the last cup is always full of grounds, which is useful if you're a fortune teller. Or you like to pick your teeth.

The Moka[2] is fun—a poor man's espresso for a person-and-a-half—but you have to be vigilant: it can explode right there on the stove, and even when it doesn't, for not even eight ounces, it's a drag to clean.[3]

---

[1] A glass carafe, invented by a chemist—Dr. Peter Schlumbohm—in 1941 (featured at MoMA in 1943), in which you make and serve your coffee. All you need is a double-sided filter and it's ready to go.

[2] Another "time-honored classic," a stove-top brewer invented by Luigi di Ponti in 1933, then made famous by Alfonso Bialetti, and, like the Chemex, displayed in museums as a triumph of design.

[3] We once stayed for a month with a couple who made two little pots every morning, very civilized, almost like one of those boutique hotels. Enchanted as I was with their arrangement, I came home and bought two for us, the regular size, and a large-scale model, which, four years later, I haven't yet tried. (Meanwhile, our former hosts have divorced. Who got custody of the Mokas? I couldn't say.)

Re Mr. Coffee and all he's inspired: it wouldn't occur to me to buy anything we'd have to plug in—to relinquish control in that way, who would do such a thing, even for the sake of consistency and precision, not I. Although this morning I'm really considering whether or not to get a scale; so as to measure out just exactly the right amount of beans; in anticipation of also getting the ratio of grounds to water exactly right (there is an equation, though the figures would have to vary, wouldn't they, according to the type of bean, not to mention personal taste. Who's accounting for personal taste, if you please? And how is that done?): till I do get that scale, if I do, I'm all about scoops—scooping without weighing and measuring—amateur-time, you don't have to tell me, I know.

On top of which, counting to thirty aside, I can't be sure about the temperature of the water, can I? So while I'm at it, I should get myself one of those kettles, the ones with a preset thermometer, so as not to leave anything to chance.

But, but, but, she sputtered, what if I want to leave something to chance?

And so I'm resisting. As I have so many times resisted instructions and directions and a thorough understanding of the task at hand—mostly because I'm lazy, okay, and also, in this case—re coffee—I'm tired of shelling out money; plus, there are aesthetic considerations: my countertops are crowded! And I like my old kettle! I like it fine! I don't want that dealie-with-the-digital-thingie on the side. And that's not all either—my reluctance goes deeper still.

It's not only that all this equipment shouldn't be necessary. Haven't people been making coffee for almost a thousand years? Wouldn't the Ethiopians laugh at this stuff? *They* roast the beans in a pan on the stove, grind them with a mortar and pestle, brew them in a special ceramic pot—a jebena—and, if the coffee's not ready, see YouTube,[4] they pour it right back and keep boiling till it is. How do they know? From the smell, from the color, from the speed of the trickle or stream. Meanwhile, we've come up with all these rules. Which just seems fussy. And fetishistic somehow. Still, you ask—don't think I'm not asking, too—don't you want your coffee to be all it can be?

What I want . . . (ping, ping, metaphor alert, extending and extending and extending—). What I want is to be gifted and talented, that's what I want. I want to be a witch, a wizard—a natural, in short—I want to think I don't need the accoutrements; that I can make an excellent pot of coffee all by myself, with my magic fingers, character, effervescent personality. I want to be one of those people about whom other people say, "she makes a great cup of coffee," or even, "she makes the *best* cup of coffee"—as opposed to, "she has the best coffee maker." (Ba dum bum.)

I guess I want coffee—the miracle and mystery of coffee—to remain mysterious and miraculous. That must be it.

Which is silly, I know: why would I leave my coffee to chance? Why not invest in the best equipment? Why not learn to use it? Except. Except the best coffee *isn't* the best,

---

[4] https://www.youtube.com/watch?v=t4zgoR_8UJY.

not if anyone can make it. Wasn't it Julia Child who said, "If you can read you can cook"? Easy for her. She could cook! One thing to follow directions—another to intuit your way to something delicious, amazing, one of a kind—

The best cup of coffee? It's the one that surprises, that's how good it is. Like—like new beans from a whole new farm in a whole new country. Last week, it was a blend of cherries from the Columbian Women of Pijao[5]—

Or, it's the cup that comes at just the right moment in the day, just what you wanted right then, a button or an opening (a period or an em dash), to the job finished up, or the one about to start—either way, you deserved a good cup of coffee, and it is—

Or, most gratifying of all, it's the cup you make for somebody else. And you actually witness the double take. *Such good coffee*, they say. Nothing so gratifying as that.

Bottom line: it's the coffee you know how to make (or I do—but second person works better here, no? In first, I sound like I'm showing off), because you—or we (how about "we"? The inclusive and generous, not the royal) have instincts: we have the touch. And yet. When we're in a café, and we order a coffee, it had better be good. They had better have it down to a science. Because that's their job! To make good coffee! Not mine—I'm a natural, that's all—coffee isn't my job; it's not even my passion—or at least I didn't know it was—

But such a good metaphor, right? For *everything*.

---

[5]Las Mujeres Association is a cooperative of women farmers from the town of Pijao in Quindío, Columbia, determined to raise and sustain the coffee bar, with long-term quality and financial viability in mind.

12 ALL THE THINGS YOU ARE[1]

—the song—begins like this:

> Time and again I've longed for adventure,
> Something to make my heart beat the faster,
> What did I long for, I never really knew . . .

Not about you, dear Coffee (now giving direct address a try).

Still, if the filter fits, yes? And it does, since among the things you are, literally and figuratively, is a stimulant, of course. Three fast cups of coffee might actually quicken a heart for a minute or two. But, though I know people who have given you up for just that reason, coffee isn't necessarily bad for the heart—especially not the female heart. So that's some good news.[2]

---

[1]Hammerstein and Kern, from the musical *Very Warm for May*, 1939.
[2]https://www.heart.org/en/news/2018/09/28/is-coffee-good-for-you-or-not.

Still, as non-threatening as you mostly turn out to be—even, in some instances, physically as well as psychologically beneficial[3]—your history is checkered; violent, in the past, in various places all over the world, where you've even been banned as Satanic and unhealthful[4]—

But, Coffee, you would not be quashed. Against the odds, you've continued to be something to make, to serve, to have, to hold, to sip, to slurp, to gulp, even to abandon—as if it's anyone's business whether or not we finish our coffee, as if anyone cares, there's plenty more where it came from, right? In most diners, anyway (as noted), refills are free. I remember my dad, the soul of moderation, putting his hand over his cup, to indicate he didn't want more. Whereas I can happily drink a whole pot of you all by myself. I don't, but, I'm saying, I could—no question, coffee, you're a good pick-me-up, a jump-starter to have on the fly: the confusing part, though—contradictory, counterintuitive—however motivational (catalystic!) you are, you also offer a person, this person (but not only me—it's not called a coffee break for nothing), a pause, a way to slow down; to look out the window, to stare into middle distance, to privately *con*template—

Or else to commune, to converse, to confide, to collaborate—k-k-k-k-k—which brings us to the word

---

[3] https://www.mayoclinic.org/healthy-lifestyle/nutrition-and-healthy-eating/expert-answers/coffee-and-health/faq-20058339.
[4] In Mecca, Italy, Constantinople, Sweden, and Prussia.

itself—beautiful, right? At once familiar (as butter or bread) and thrillingly exotic; maybe because, in whatever tongue, that consonant rockets off the back of the throat (the *c*ords!), to sound pretty much just like itself every time: kahvi, kaffe, café, kopi, káva, kahawa, kaffi, keopi, kāfēi[5]—and all from the original Arabic, qahwah—which tells us what? That this, at least, the music of coffee, we commonly share.

And even in plain old American English, coffee-the-word is fun to say: first that hard "c", then the generous diphthong; next the caress of that double "f"—finally the long "e", intimate, endearing. The easiest vowel to sing, by the way. And—if you're into alliteration, by now it's evident, isn't it, so many companionable (compatible) words, not to be cute, but consider: connection, communication, commiseration, consolation, candor—

Coffee, as comfort, crutch, conduit to getting things done—

Enough already, enough—what about coffee as spark or prompt? Not necessarily beginning with Gertrude Stein and her book in celebration of things (in fact, Bach's "Coffee Cantata" preceded *Tender Buttons* by almost 200 years), but worth a look, certainly—here's how Stein's poem, or whatever it is, begins:

A Piece of Coffee
More of Double
A place in no new table.

---

[5]Finnish, Swedish, French, Indonesian, Czech, Swahili, Icelandic, Korean, Mandarin.

A single image is not splendor. Dirty is yellow. A sign of more in not mentioned. A piece of coffee is not a detainer. The resemblance to yellow is dirtier and distincter. The clean mixture is whiter and not coal color, never more coal color than altogether.

I don't get it, I don't. I mean—don't think I don't I love her for "distincter." But the rest? One thing to describe a button as *tender*, enough to inspire a specialty boutique. Or at least a name for same. (Tender Buttons[6] first opened its doors in 1965.) But try to find a store called "A Piece of Coffee," or "No new table," in reference to this not very appetizing section of Gertrude Stein's book. And please to let me know if you come up with anything—I did not.

---

[6]143 East 62nd St., New York, NY.

13 THE POWER OF SUGGESTION

Somebody posts a picture on Instagram. It's a sliver of a window up high, blue sky and clouds—slightly oblong, off-center, eye-catching—the background is dark, no way of knowing what room this is or where—

It might be a cell—in a prison; or a monastery—it might be in the attic of a great old house, or in a castle (although the window is contemporary)—

And the caption: *Coffee, served with a slice of sky.* Coffee! That changes everything, right? It's not just an interesting picture anymore, it's a scene. Who wouldn't immediately start to fill in the blanks; to come up with a story to go with the image and the words? And how about the power of those words to evoke the cup of coffee that isn't in the frame?[1]

---

[1] Months later, looking at my notes for this section—a description of the photo—I wonder: can this be right? No coffee in the picture, not anywhere? I go looking on the app, but I can't seem to find it. Who'd posted the photo in the first place, why didn't I make a note of *that*? But I think I remember

Which reminds me, bear with me, of Achilles G. Rizzoli, the artist who was trained as an architectural draftsman, whose drawings of buildings turn out to be portraits of people, that's how they're titled, anyway, right there on the canvas or whatever, in beautiful lettering: *Mr. and Mrs. Harold Nealy Symbolically Sketched* (a cathedral); *Gerry George Gould Holt A Scholar and a Gentleman* (a university building, impressive, imposing); and a few of the palaces go by *Mother Symbolically Represented*. Sometimes he elaborates, calligraphically—as in *A Picture of My Beautiful, Beautiful Mother*—in case we, or she, didn't get it, quite.

What I'm thinking—you could show me a picture of just about anything, any place, person, vista, call it coffee; that would work for me. As photogenic as coffee is all by itself, as many shots as I've snapped—cups, mugs, pots, beans, grounds, drips, dregs, and so on—couldn't a caption convince you they were pictures of places? Paris, New York, Echo Park? Or people? (Or moods? #Mood—I wouldn't have to do

---

it was Sonja Livingston, a splendid writer whom I slightly know (though we've never met face-to-face), and I email to ask: *Sonja, did you once post a photo with the caption "coffee served with a slice of sky"? I want to give credit where credit is due.* Sonja writes back: *Coffee and slices of sky belong to all of us. Post away!* I explain then, I'm not posting, I'm quoting—may I quote her, please? She looks back to find the image—it was hers, I was right, photo and caption—and sends it along. And it's just as I'd originally described-but-didn't-finally-remember it: no cup of coffee lurking in a corner (like Bonnard's little black cat, in *The Open Window*, 1921); only that rectangle of marbled sky. Talk about the power of suggestion.

more than that.) As for my photos of anything but: if I were to caption them "coffee with . . ." I might have us seeing— imagining, eventually remembering—a dimension that just isn't there. As with that instagram post: *Coffee served with a slice of sky.* Don't you visualize the steam curling out of the mug? And smell the brew? And regret your own day getting swallowed up much too fast? Oh, to have another slice of sky and drink it, too.

Speaking of which, for days now, Carly Simon has been in my head—clouds in my coffee, clouds in my coffee—I'm belting it out when Fred asks if I know the story of the song. The story of the song? You mean about Warren Beatty? No, no, he says—

What he heard, is that Bob Dylan and Carly Simon were talking—were having coffee together (on an ocean liner, he thinks, but maybe I should look that part up), when Bob told Carly you can write a song about anything: "Like this cup of coffee," he said. It was a kind of challenge. Or contest. And that's how we got Simon's "You're so vain," says Fred, and Dylan's "One More Cup of Coffee"—

And what a good story, right? I can't find it anywhere. Did you Google "One Cup of Coffee"? Fred asks. Of course I did. How about Dylan and Simon on an ocean liner? Yes, I Googled that, too. "I couldn't have made this up," Fred says.

If he did, if he didn't, I like it—I like it enough to repeat it. I like that neither song is about coffee at all: coffee (any way you slice it) is a very good prompt. Take a picture of love, requited or not, call it coffee, go ahead. Or vice versa—forget the woman in her robe: picture her Picardie glass instead, a bare thing (but full of coffee, of course) sitting on the table just there. Caption it, *Woman in her Robe*; or even *Beautiful, beautiful woman in her robe* (the power of suggestion); or (forget the woman) how about *This morning, this day, this life*—but that's so on the nose, isn't it? Maybe some lines from the Dylan would do—how about this:

One more cup of coffee for the road
One more cup of coffee fore I go
To the valley below.

14 ONE MORE PROMPT

From poet Ron Padgett—

The title is actually "Prose Poem ("The morning coffee.")," and it starts like this:

> The morning coffee. I'm not sure why I drink it. Maybe it's the ritual/of the cup, the spoon, the hot water, the milk, and the little heap of/brown grit, the way they come together to form a nail I can hang the/day on. [. . .]

Writers: on your marks, get set, go!

The morning coffee. I know exactly why I drink it. What I have been going on about, yeesh. But truly, if I didn't have this means of re-entry—slow, steady, familiar—a way to paddle over the dream-line and into the day—if instead I were to purchase that speedboat I saw at Sur La Table the other afternoon—

"This is the Moccamaster," said the woman in the store apron. "If you like pour-over coffee, this is for you, makes a perfect cup every time—weighs, measures, calibrates the ratios, adjusts the temp—it does *everything*—"

Everything, apparently, but fetch the paper and read the headlines (so I don't have to).

Reminds me, the Moccamaster does, of our master bedroom toilet, now unplugged. But hooked up, I swear, it did everything but make the morning coffee. My daughter and her wife installed it when I broke my elbows (both of them, yes), which was great at the time, the toilet, I mean, but now that I can flush by myself again, so I will till I can't, thank you very much—a person likes a little control. But we were talking about coffee—we were nodding to a poet, and now, just look, poetry sacrificed entirely, and—all this talk of toilets—I've probably ruined your coffee, besides. Where was I? Re-entering that's where. Pouring and checking the color of the drip—like watching the dawn (which I do at the very same time) wash the sky from purple to pink to white.

Of course Padgett's coffee—the speaker's coffee, I mean, is instant—he tells us so somewhere in the middle:

Surely there's something better to do, though, than to
drink a cup of/instant coffee. Such as meditate? About

what? About having a cup of/coffee. A cup of coffee
whose first drink is too hot and whose last drink/is too
cool, but whose many in-between drinks are, like Baby
Bear's por-/ridge, just right. [. . .]

And then the poem takes a turn. Papa breaks his cup and
makes a mess.

"In a way," writes Padgett, "it's good that Mama
Bear isn't there. Better that she rest/in her grave beyond the
garden, unaware of what has happened to the/world."

To the world. Not just here in the kitchen. Papa reads the
newspaper, too.

But see what a prompt can do? From coffee to grief, just
like that. First thought, off the top of my head (after I bemoan
the instant coffee): Who will I be when my mother isn't here
to tell me what she thinks of the world? What she thinks
of me. (Whether or not I agree.) And another on its heels:
What about when *I'm* dead? How can it be I won't know
what my children are saying and doing and thinking and
remembering? How not to wonder what they will *remember*?
How not to want to make it good?

15 AM I BLUE

Once upon a time I was a hostess in a restaurant on the Upper East side, one of those places that catered to two different crowds, the hip and well-heeled (yuppies, we used to call them—bankers, lawyers, drinkers), from happy hour to well after midnight; and, between eleven and three, the blue-hairs—back when henna was as crazy as we got with color, and that blue wasn't strictly intentional. Day after day in they came, the ladies who lunched, in parties of three and four and more, all dressed up, matching shoes and bags, and they had their favorite tables and dishes and servers, as in:

Where's that nice boy? The one who was here yesterday?

And (reproachfully):
No, dear, by the window, I always sit there, you know that—

And (alarmed):
What do you mean you don't have the chicken salad? Well. You'll have to bring me the club. With an extra piece of bacon. The cobb for me. And coffee. Who else wants coffee? Coffee for me.

I'll have the sole. No almonds. And coffee.

Pie for me, just pie. And coffee, of course. Sweetheart, you know what? Bring me a scoop of vanilla on the side, will you, please?[1]

And, on one particular day:

Young man! (To the waiter, another nice boy who just happened to be my little brother;[2] I'd gotten him the job)— *Young man, do I know you? Are you new? I don't think I know you.*

I guess not, said my-brother-the-waiter, probably trying to smile. Or at least not to spit.

Well, I want coffee, said the blue-hair. *I want it hot, I want it black, I want it now,* she said.

My brother wasn't, still isn't, like me. He didn't need anyone's approval. He wasn't susceptible to the bullying (or the subsequent flattery), which, in my case, went something like this: *We'll have that table, darling* (gesturing to prime real estate smack in the middle of the dining room). *No, I said that one.* Stopped dead now, vigorously pointing this time,

---

[1] No such thing as an *affogato* back then, not at McMullen's on 77th and Third. But that's why she wanted the ice cream, not for the pie, but to "drown" it. In coffee. "*Affogato*" for drowned (in Italian), also the name of the now-very-trendy dessert: vanilla ice cream with a shot of espresso. And, another shot, too, if you like, of your favorite liqueur.

[2] Not the one with the grinder. The other one. Who also loves coffee, but because it interfered with his sleep, has pretty much given it up for black tea.

resisting a four-top in the corner. By a window. In the back. (She used to like the window, but she knew, she'd figured it out: I was saving the more visible table, per instructions from my boss, for a less venerable party—as in lither, leaner, leggier, with at least one natural blond.[3]) If and when I surrendered, she'd pat my arm ever so sweetly. *You're a good girl*, she'd say, or something like that. Which would set me up for the rest of day. Not so my little brother.

On the shift I'm remembering, back in the kitchen, he put a cup of coffee, already hot, in the microwave for two full minutes. Delivered it without a word. The blue-hair burned her tongue, of course, and over this, my brother nearly lost the job.[4] I begged on his behalf—it would not happen again, I promised. I made him promise, too.

But secretly I was proud of him. Shame on that blue-hair—to be honest, I don't recall if hers was actually blue,

---

[3]Blondes are maybe not the best advertising now, but in the 80s, on the Upper East Side . . .

[4]Wouldn't you know, my brother remembers "the hot coffee and the blue-hairs," but, according to him, that wasn't the day I bailed him out. It was the time when a bunch of guys—young and raucous—paid their check as if to free up the table, then ordered another round. "I gave them a look," he says: they were the ones who'd complained. And what *I* did then? I told him he'd better apologize. If anyone else were on duty, I said, he might have been fired. In short, though I've cast myself as a hero, I didn't save the day, that's revisionist history—I only scolded, as big sisters do. The thing is, I still don't recall his version. But am I so sure of my own? I'll tweak, I tell him. "Not on my account," he says. And he adds: "My memory ain't what it used to be." (Point taken.)

but very possibly it was; the blue rinse, meant to counter the yellow in a head full of gray or white (made famous by Jean Harlow, and later Queen Elizabeth[5]) was all the rage for the over-sixty set. That's why we called them the *blue-hairs*, shame on all of them, pushing us around.

Listen to me, like all this happened yesterday—no less righteous, no less indignant. Also, check out my hair. A few years ago the gray began to come in, not so much, but since it was happening, why not have a little fun, I decided, and I went for blue (really blue), a streak here and there, to shine up my natural espresso and bring out the silver; that's the idea anyway, and it's subtle, I promise. You wouldn't notice unless I brought it up. Unless we were walking in the sun and I showed you: Look, see? What do you think, how do you like it? Funny, I might say, I'm one of the blue-hairs now. For real.

---

[5] According to Wikipedia, where I learned that Netanyahu is a blue-hair, too. Though usually the term applies to women. In England, the blue-hairs, generally older, well-heeled, conservative, devoted to charity, are known as the "Blue Rinse Brigade."

FROM THE COFFEE DIARIES #3

I hate the new grinder. This morning I found myself cleaning it, piece by piece, including the piece that isn't supposed to get wet, and I got it wet; and I've turned it upside down so many times, which is also ill-advised ("Never turn your grinder upside down," says the know-it-all on YouTube) . . .

What I'm longing to do is to return to the old grinder. The inferior little grinder with the single blade, which couldn't possibly produce a good cup of coffee, no way, in your dreams, so I'm told, so then why was the coffee so good?

16 A WORD ABOUT TEA

An acquaintance writes in an email: "No one ever goes for 'a quick cup of tea.' A quick cup of coffee, yes. Tea, no. God, I hate tea," he adds. And then: "Here's another thing: the British morphed 'tea' into a word for yet another meal. That would never happen to 'coffee.'"

True that. Coffee is not a meal. It's *with* a meal, or *after* a meal, or *instead* of a meal—it's a way to get by or through, a quick fix; whereas tea, just logistically speaking, unless it's cold in a pitcher in the fridge, has to steep for a bit, doesn't it? And that slows things down. Right, too, that "tea" comes at the end of the day—afternoon tea, with little sandwiches and cakes on a three-tiered platter, or else, high tea, aka supper on the early side: bangers and beans. Welsh rarebit. A hearty soup and maybe some pudding.[1]

These days, though, coffee, depending where you are, might also require forbearance. "Come *on*," groans a friend,

---

[1] A catch-all Britishism for dessert.

who can't abide the new deal at a local café, "this business of making each cup, one at a time . . ." She doesn't want to watch the drip, drip, drip. She isn't seduced. She wants her coffee, hot, black, now. "How can people stand it?" she says. "To pay five bucks to wait 20 minutes for a damn Americano!" It's our expectations that get in our way: in our mind's eye we can see the old coffee machine by the waiters' station in our favorite Greek diner, those refills coming at us fast as we can drink them. But isn't it lovely to order coffee after dinner, and have it arrive in a mini-French press? "Just wait three minutes or so," the waiter instructs.

And there was one occasion, before an event at a gallery downtown—we'd arrived early, and so stopped for Vietnamese coffees to kill a little time. Having never had one before, I was captivated by the tiny tin pot and filter (like a Moka!), the coffee so inky, dripping into an inch and a half of what looked like custard—condensed milk, it was, and sweetened, too.

"How do we drink this?" I asked the waiter.
"Be patient," he said.

What I'm admitting here: when my friend looks at the clock and complains, I make the right noises, but I'm only pretending to sympathize. Coffee and sympathy isn't a thing, after all. It's *tea* and sympathy—everybody knows that. Tea is friendly enough, but benign. Non-judgmental. Whereas coffee is exciting, dangerous (not because it's actually dangerous!²), date-worthy even, a gesture of interest, an opening, a prelude to the next thing, and the thing after that—

Someone offers you tea? It's because you're ill, or sad, or wrapping things up. Tea is safe. Tea is for the end of the day. With exceptions, of course. (As noted) there are those who've replaced the morning coffee with a pot of black tea, or even the green kind, or red—or turmeric, or mint; that's the other thing: tea can be made out of just about anything; add hot water to anything at all, and what do you have? Some kind of tea! Mint tea, green tea, ginger tea, chamomile, licorice, apple, maple, peach, honey-lemon—tip of the berg. Tea doesn't discriminate—nor can one afford to be a snob about tea, not really. Or maybe one can. One can sniff, I suppose, if it isn't Harrods, or Twinings, or PG Tips (one friend, in response to my questionnaire, had nothing whatever to say about coffee: "Now if you'd asked about PG Tips," she wrote)—or, maybe, no matter the brand, one objects to bags altogether, and only drinks tea from a beautiful tin, loose, steeped, cozied. Coffee, though, whatever it evokes (honeydew, sweet pine, golden raisins), is always coffee.

---

²It's good for us, remember? "Coffee consumption" among other benefits, and in addition to increasing sperm motility and mitigating migraines, "can apparently help prevent Parkinson's, Alzheimer's, liver cancer, colon cancer, type 2 diabetes, and gallstones," writes coffee authority Mark Pendergrast in *Uncommon Grounds: The History of Coffee and How it Transformed our World* (Basic Books, 2010) (pp. 377–8).

In conclusion: tea and sympathy, coffee and company—unless. Unless, as previously discussed, that cup of coffee is a calculated solitary pleasure or strategy, having to do with a sense of mission accomplished or renewed. Whereas tea is medicinal: for the upset stomach, the cough, the bad throat, the broken heart. And tea bags for weary, teary eyes. Moreover, tea can be weak. But if coffee is weak, it's no good! Who wants a weak cup of coffee, who would ever ask for such a thing?

So tea is more flexible, maybe. More accommodating, less hard to fuck up—but coffee, if riskier, is sexier, too. And there's this, from artist Robert Rauschenberg, all over the internet: *I've had cold coffee and hot coffee, good coffee and lousy coffee, but I've never had a sad cup of coffee.*

Although, as excited as I was when I found the quote, come to find out he didn't mean it quite the way it sounds: *not* to cheer us, *not* to recommend. Rather, supposedly, he was taking aim at Allen Ginsberg's "Howl," in which Ginsberg purportedly referenced "the sad cup of coffee"—and isn't this a sign of the times, all of us quoting out of context. For our own purposes. On top of which, there's no such phrase in "Howl." No mention at all of coffee, not that I can find. So if Rauschenberg said this, what did he mean? If he didn't say it, who did? It's such a great line, goes so well with my thesis, serves my purposes—

Except what sort of silly argument am I making? As if it's a contest—coffee or tea—as if we have to declare ourselves. We do not. Happy or miserable, we can have both. We can like both.

And, listen to this—it's in the middle of this writing, no kidding, that my son, who's come over to do laundry, and is puttering around overhead, calls down to ask if I want a cup of tea.

I maybe want coffee later, I say. You go ahead, okay?

I'll have coffee, he says.

No, no, I say, it's okay, go ahead, have tea.

But the point is to have something together, he says.

So, up the stairs I come singing:

> I love coffee, I love tea,
> I love the java jive and it loves me,
> Coffee and tea and the java and me,
> A cup, a cup, a cup, a cup, a cup (boy!) . . .[3]

---

[3]From "Java Jive," by Ben Oakland and Milton Drake, 1940.

A RIDDLE (EXCELLENT ADVERTISING)

I'm not going to tell you the name of this coffee—you have to guess.

First clue: it's serious. Earnest, even stern—not what you'd associate with anything appetizing, not at first; its connotations are righteous; it brings to mind Sundays—discipline, accountability, guidance, direction. You don't want that kind of coffee? You don't need a lecture? But hold on now, don't be so quick to reject a little wisdom: pull the bag from the shelf. Have a longer look. Check out the fine print. Along with the rigor, you can expect to take home the following: "chocolate, blueberry pie, velvety . . ."

Isn't that genius? Starting with the candy—plain, straight-ahead—no distractions. Then the pastry: the promise of not only fruit, but crust, baked and buttery, extra effort and care implied. Expertise, too—the texture, if flaky, will be smoother than smooth (like velvet): I'm salivating here. Don't know about you, I have to try this coffee.

Name this coffee![1]

(What, you wouldn't buy it for the label on the bag? I would. I did.)

---

[1] It's Sermon from Verve.

FROM THE COFFEE DIARIES #4

If American Airlines texts at three a.m. to cancel your civilized midmorning flight, and you have to rearrange in the dark, and you never really get back to sleep, and you get to the airport just barely in time to make the new flight (at the proverbial crack), and then you have to sit in a middle seat between a Republican and a very large man who won't give up an inch of the arm rest; and if, once you finally pick up your luggage (the last to come out), it takes ages to rent a damn car, and ages-some-more to get out of the city and onto the highway (by which time it's dusk with a three-hour ride still ahead); and if then, at a drive-through, your husband pays for two coffees, but, while he's waiting for change, takes a call and drives away with the money but not with the drinks (even though you're madly gesturing—but he waves you off and keeps talking), and once back on the highway you can't turn around (and though he's sweetly contrite, you're not about to give him a break, and you're both just fried and full of despair), and if, just about then (what, ho! Behold!), he sees another drive-through just up the road, and, just in time, pulls off the exit and into the line, only two cars ahead of you, and orders and pays and waits for the coffees this time—I'm telling you, A, he's your hero and B, a macchiato from Dunkin Donuts is ambrosial, period the end.

17 REUNION

We met in Arlington, at the Starbucks on Mass Ave. He looked exactly the same, but different, his hair, for one thing, so meticulously parted and combed, and he so conservatively dressed, as if impersonating a partner in a law firm on his day off (which, granted, he is—a partner—but was it the weekend? Can't remember—), in pressed pants, and a polo and a navy blue crewneck. I wanted to reach out and mess with his do, me in my baggy red pants and a long-sleeved T, wishing I were thinner, wishing I were prettier—wishing both of us had known how pretty I used to be, hoping I was holding up all right; suspecting, I wasn't, no more than he. How do you hold up after thirty-plus years? (And this is the thing about running into people decades after the fact—if they look sort of awful, chances are you do, too).

It was because he'd written a few months earlier to say "if you're ever nearby," and "I'd like to be in touch," that we'd arranged to meet. He'd lost someone to AIDS—a guy I'd known a little, and admired—the loss had reminded him; had made him think, he said, that he hadn't been a very good friend. True that. In the interim, my father, a disgraced (ultimately vindicated) politico-turned-restaurateur, had been murdered. I should have heard from this guy when it happened. At the time I even wrote to him and his wife, only to get a card back from her—*So sorry for your loss*—nothing more. Now to be big enough not to ask, *how could you, why didn't you.* And somehow I was; somehow I managed to say only that I was glad to hear from him. I'd let him know, I said, when were in the 'hood. And eventually we were.

I got there first, to the Starbucks—chose a table, took a seat. A mistake, I thought, when he pulled out the chair across from me. Too much natural light—any actor worth her on-camera scene study class is obliged to be aware of these things—I only realized (too late) when I saw him see me through the window. But that was why I'd chosen the spot in the first place, to be able to see him come in.

All told, we spent less than a hour. Three decades since the last time we'd met—in Boston, as couples, just before they got married. Four kids between us, all nearly grown. So there should have been plenty—too much—to catch up on, though honestly, in the first twenty minutes, I learned more than I wanted to. That his second wife is twenty-five years younger than he (in a photo, I'd supposed she was his daughter); that they have a place in the North End looking out on what? The harbor? Can that be right? I ought to remember, he made a point of the view. Also of his weekend retreat, several acres not far from the city. He'd just put in an orchard, he said— apples and pears—beautiful, idyllic, I should just see. He leaned forward as he told me all this: Was I getting it? How well things had turned out? If anyone should get it, would get it, it would have to be me. At last, he tipped back in his chair. The first wife had made him miserable, he said. He'd been so lonely in that marriage, he guessed he deserved some happiness now.

How to assure him I was pleased (not surprised; that wouldn't do) except to say so straight out? And why did the words sound canned, if not to him (hopefully not to him), to me? It's not like I didn't mean what I said. Only whatever his original impulse—to make amends, I'd thought—he'd forgotten to ask about us: my husband, my kids, my work. Or maybe he didn't forget. Maybe I should cut him some slack. How to frame such questions thirty years out—how to ask if a life can resume a natural pace in the wake of unnatural circumstances? (It can, though. It can, it does, it happens all the time.) But by then I'd realized: the urgency he'd felt about getting together for coffee had little to do with me, really; he had his own feelings to speak.[1] So I was startled, jolted, slightly, when he finally blurted, "I remember your dad really well."

He reminded me they'd met a couple of times—that on one occasion my father had advised him to go into the restaurant business: "People have to eat. That's what he told me."

"Spoken like a man disbarred," I joked, but he didn't laugh.

"I met your grandfather, too, remember?" I nodded even though I didn't.

---

[1] A go-to phrase between Freddy and me, since I played Teresa in John Patrick Shanley's *Italian American Reconciliation*. There's a scene, very funny: she and Huey, her boyfriend, are arguing, and she tells him: "I can't be only watching out for your feelings, Sweetheart. I've got my own feelings to speak."

"I'll never forget him," he said.

No reason, no room for me to explain that the father hadn't been well enough to take in the son's violent end. Had died, himself, not long after, in a demented rage. My old boyfriend rightly recalled that my grandfather, brilliant and wise, was my hero back then. He—Grandpa, I mean—had apparently noted at the time that responsibilities, "which I couldn't imagine ever having," said the buttoned-up executive, a man with multiple wives, and children, and abodes, "are like barnacles. You don't notice you've acquired them, but there they are."

Ah ha. No wonder he needed me to know he has an orchard. And a view.

Meanwhile, nothing coming back to me, not about either of those visits with either of those giants gone missing. How can that be, that one person remembers so vividly, the other not at all? How did those men—my father, my grandfather—get to my boyfriend in a way they never got to me? Or did they. Wouldn't I love to meet them for coffee. To tell them how things have turned out. Some things. Others not so much, but no point in upsetting anyone—plus, I'm as self-absorbed as the next guy (this guy I've been talking about)—which is why, if I met them at Starbucks, Grandpa and Dad (if only), I might well forget, or even choose not to ask how they've been since they died, and all-dead ever since.

Oof, talk about a sad cup of coffee. Whatever he had in mind when he said it, Rauschenberg was wrong.

COFFEE AND MY FATHER[1]

I don't remember how my father took his coffee, not really, but I want to think he drank it black—of course he did. Who to ask? Nobody to ask. Nobody to ask about my father and his coffee—

Well, let me try to remember—am I making this up?—so strong is my sense of his presence, his voice, I can hear it still, coming from the kitchen, where he talked on the phone; and read the paper; and drank his coffee—his *black* coffee—

Or from the patio, where he lounged, sunning himself—talking on the phone; reading the paper; drinking coffee, more coffee, definitely black—

And I remember him taking me out to lunch, watching me eat, a grilled cheese sandwich every time—with potato

---

[1]My "real" father, I called him. "Biological," was a mouthful, and too scientific to me. Misleading, besides—he wasn't only that. Although "real" was also wrong, as if to imply that my stepfather wasn't, when, in truth, nobody was more of a father, more present, more real to me, than he.

chips or French fries or onion rings (all forbidden foods at home)—and a milkshake or a frappe. If he ate, too, but usually he didn't, but if he did, say, order a tuna on rye, it went down in two bites, I swear, just two. Then: Coffee, he'd say to the waitress. Cream? she'd ask, glancing up from her pad. Because his voice was so deep? Because he was handsome and monosyllabic?

Black, he'd say again, without looking at her. Black, for sure, no question about it, I knew it, I did. And—this I also know—he never said please. Or thank you. Only, *Coffee, black.*

FROM THE COFFEE DIARIES #5

As with all the dreams, I'm some version of lost, in this case on a freeway, behind the wheel, but it's not the right freeway, and the angle is extreme, and I'm sliding and sliding, and it's hailing, I realize, and my wheels can't get any traction and, the thing is, I have Mr. Coffee, the machine, beside me (I remind you, I have never owned such a thing), riding shotgun, plugged in, and I'm actually happy, in the dream, to note that it's brewing nicely, not spilling, never mind the pitch of the road—

So that's something anyway—whatever else happens, if I happen to crash, at least there will be coffee; except I notice, veering toward an exit or entrance to yet another narrow expressway, that I only used a couple of scoops, oh no, oh no, there's too much water, the coffee will be weak—

No time like the present to wake myself up. And make it right.

FROM THE COFFEE DIARIES #6

If you like the morning, or you don't—how to begin with anything other than coffee? My college roommate used to drink Tab. Always a twelve-pack of Tab on the floor of our off-campus kitchen. Even now I have a friend—she drinks her first Diet Coke before 8 a.m. Another has given up coffee for a muddy, medicinal substitute. Because her acupuncturist told her that coffee is bad, bad, bad. As noted, my own brother drinks tea—coffee makes him anxious, he says. And there's my therapist—I sent her the questionnaire. She never got around to filling it out. "Dinah, if you'd asked me about bunnies," she said, so contrite. (She has a couple of adorable rabbits in a pen in her dining room.) Coffee, however? No love lost there. Coffee gave her arrhythmia, she says.

"Coffee did?" I ask. Coffee wouldn't do that, not coffee, oh no—
"Well—coffee and black tea."
"They gave you *arrhythmia*?"

"Well, not coffee, exactly—"

She can see that I'm upset on her behalf. On behalf of coffee as well. I'm shaking my head in disbelief.

"Not coffee," she clarifies, "caffeine."

"Arrhythmia. Wow."

"I had to take medication," she says.

I want to tell her: *Let me make you a cup of coffee. My coffee won't give you arrhythmia, I promise it won't.*

But OK. If you don't drink coffee, whoever you are, it isn't your fault, it isn't a fault at all, it's fine (you're only mildly suspect as far as I'm concerned). Still, it's amazing what people will eat and drink first thing in the morning. I once had a houseguest, in town on business, ask for a carrot for breakfast. A raw carrot. Washed but unpeeled. To go with a strong cup of coffee, at least, so that made me feel marginally better about sending him into his day.

18 COFFEE AND CATASTROPHE

One of those mornings, portentous, dread-full. A sickly sky, as happens in September in LA, when the wind singes, and the light is yellow-weird more days than it isn't. The kind of weather, wrote Raymond Chandler, that's enough to make "[m]eek little wives feel the edge of the carving knife and study their husbands' necks"[1]—that line always comes to mind when the Santa Anas blow. But on this day, something else in the air, something frightening and foul: what was it Hillary said, exactly? (I'm looking it up.) "I'm the last thing standing between you and the apocalypse."[2] And that's how it feels—that's how it felt, stationed in front of the TV. Before

---

[1]From the story "Red Wind," published in the eponymous collection in 1946. The passage starts like this: "It was one of those hot dry Santa Anas that come down through the mountain passes and curl your hair and make your nerves jump and your skin itch."
[2]https://www.nytimes.com/2016/10/16/magazine/hillary-clinton-campaign-final-weeks.html.

breakfast. (Not a good sign.) Drinking coffee, of course. Waiting for Christine Blasey Ford.

When she arrived—spectacled, in professional navy blue—how brave she seemed, how poised, albeit apprehensive. First, Senator Grassley went on and on; then Senator Feinstein went on and on; then, before Dr. Ford could begin, Grassley asked if she needed anything.

"I think after reading my opening statement, I anticipate needing some caffeine if that is available," she said.

She spoke then for almost twenty minutes, maintaining her composure throughout. At the end she said (again), ". . . at this point, I will do my best to answer your questions, and would request some caffeine." Someone asked if a coke would do. A coke? For a grown woman? At 9 a.m.? But Ford didn't flinch; she was only polite, or possibly desperate. Or a little of both. "That sounds good," she said. "That would be great, thanks."

While Grassley stated the ground rules, a preamble to the hired prosecutor's interrogation, someone (Cory Booker it was later reported) brought the witness (the *patriot*)—who was about to be interrogated as if she were the one to have committed a crime—what appeared to be a cup of coffee. At that point, wrapping up his remarks, Grassley said, "Dr. Ford, I'm told you want a break right now, and if you do, that's fine."

"I'm okay," said Dr. Ford, opening a sugar pack into the Styrofoam cup. "I got the coffee. I think I can proceed and sip on the coffee."

One of her lawyers whispered something in her ear, looked like maybe he was letting her know there was a stirrer on the other side of the cup. But Ford was respectfully focused on Grassley—so the other lawyer, the woman on her right, picked up the stick and did the stirring. Then Grassley said something about how Dr. Ford was fortunate because "nobody can mix up [his] coffee right." And everyone chuckled, she too, cooperative, courteous, behaving like a woman, as women are taught to behave, because if she were perceived to be emotional or hysterical—or anything less than eager to please—she'd be accused, wouldn't she, of behaving like a woman—?

But, honestly, Mr. Senator, talk about choice of words: Dr. Ford was *fortunate* that morning? Because someone managed to "mix up [her] coffee right?" Who says? Who says they got it right? I know, I know, avuncular you, you were making a joke, you were trying to dispel the tension in the room—but *fortunate*? I don't think so. We, the American people, *might* have been fortunate—

But Christine Blasey Ford? If she made a difference that morning—and I want to believe she did—she sacrificed her fortune, didn't she, to a cruel mix-up, which also isn't the word; no mix-up there. Only blatant contempt for women, for justice, for truth. To pretend to have watched and listened and heard, or *not* heard what she plainly said; to go on to ignore her testimony—as devastating as it was professional— no question as to her credibility; no question she'd put the fate of the nation over her own. And yet, Mr. Grassley et al., you wound up rewarding *him*—puerile, shrill, rude, emotional, hysterical (but in a man, such qualities apparently demonstrate reserves of righteousness and passion)—tell me, please, what's the word for *that*?

Galling, there's one. Galling, grievous, monstrous, appalling, disgusting—there's a parade. What could we do? We made more and more coffee. And I wound up crying (so angry was I, even before Kavanaugh's turn). But Dr. Ford held strong, though she hardly touched her Styrofoam cup. After a break, she switched it out for a bottle of coke after all. Maybe she prefers a cold soda—some people do, okay. Whatever the case, my guess, Senator Grassley? That there was one feeble cup of Joe, disingenuous, insincere, altogether lousy, in keeping with the outcome of the day.

FROM THE COFFEE DIARIES #7

[In which—very unusual owing to an early appointment on the other side of town, I order a coffee, my first of the day, outside.]

This latte is enough to make me rethink my whole life. There's the fact that it comes in a highball glass[1], looks like a parfait; plus the foam, whipped and balanced just so, two inches, I'd say, on top of the rest, resisting the spoon—or is it inviting me to take the plunge? As in, dig away, eat me like meringue, like frosting, like flan—

Whatever its agenda I'm paralyzed: what to do, how to handle this exquisite confection, how to be in the moment, how?

And this is when I realize: I avoid stirring, always I do. Not at home—at home there's no need to stir, nothing to avoid. What I do at home is heat the milk first, and then fill

---

[1] I will, the very next day, start drinking my coffee from a tumbler, a tall one in the mornings, the short kind in the afternoons.

the cup (and I don't use sugar, not ever). My coffee at home doesn't preen, doesn't make demands. Leaves me free to existentially roam, to forget where I am; to find myself asking myself, what happened to the time, where did it go? Whereas, this coffee calls for action—this coffee has consequences: I can sit here and appreciate its beauty until it gets cold; or I can drink it right down.

Either way casts me as a spoiler, though: and this is why I don't like to stir, I knew there was a reason, but is it also a character flaw? Never *mind* my wandering mind (I'm working on that—although what good is staying present, as it were, if it causes consternation and doubt?); am I overly invested in appearances? Lacking the courage of my convictions? Afraid (metaphor alert!) that this coffee cannot possibly taste as good as it looks?

19 COFFEE IN ECHO PARK

Back in the 80s, there was only the Brite Spot, on Sunset, a mile and a half away.

Now, there's Pollen (formerly FIX) at the bottom of our hill. (They have a swell turmeric black pepper latte.)

Also on Echo Park Ave., at the corner of Effie, less than a half a mile down, Valerie. A snotty little place, but they make excellent scrambled eggs, and I like their jellies and jams.

A bit further on, and also on the west side of the street, there used to be Chango.

Chango, more than any of the others, made me feel old, everyone tatted up and pierced and skinny and pale and looking like he/she/they could use a sandwich. Truth be known, I hardly ever went there. And now it's changed hands: it's a "plant-based deli" called Counterpart, where, so they tell me, you can get a credible vegan pastrami on rye. Glowing Juices is next door (they both sell coffee, of course); and then comes Cookbook, a grocery. (Rumor is, Sightglass Coffee—based in San Francisco—created a blend, Blueboon, just for them.)

But to say how things have changed in the 'hood. When we first moved in there was a huge Chinese market on Sunset, a few blocks east, cheap and abundant, and nobody spoke much English, or could translate the various labels, but they had tubs full of fish, all kinds—eels squirming in a barrel, that kind of thing; and aisle after aisle of produce and condiments, soy by the vat, rice by the bushel; and cooking equipment, strainers, skimmers, fryers, double-boilers. For ages, it was bustling and noisy, that place, though last time I went in, the stock was scanty, and a year ago they gave up and closed. Nothing new in the space, not yet—but we can dream, can't we? Let's see . . . Over twenty years ago, our Eliza, age seven or eight, stood in line to sit on Santa's lap. Little girl after little girl asked for Barbie—or her house, or her car—Barbie this, Barbie that. Finally it was Lizie's turn. "What would you like for Christmas, little girl?" asked Santa. "Anything but Barbie," she answered. This is a long way of getting around to what we want in that big empty store. Anything but coffee.

Granted, we love coffee. (Barbie not so, not ever, she never did catch on around here.) But so many specialty coffee venues already, look at them all: Stories Cafe (connected to the bookstore), Triniti, Woodcut, Eightfold, Winsome, Hi Honey, Konbi, Starbucks (it's a Reserve, I think)—all less than a mile away. And the Beacon in the boathouse down at the lake. Then, within two miles or so: Intelligentsia, Dinosaur, La Colombe, Tierra Mia, Dayglow, Foxhole, Muddy Paw, Street Level, Go Get Em Tiger, Café Tropical—there are more, too. It's hard to keep track.

And—about Counterpart—that vegan alternative on Echo Park Ave.: they are also not alone, far from it. Off the top of my head, there's Elf, Lento, Little Pine, Chloe, and Sage—with an ice cream counter in the offing. Sage came first. Jake was home on winter break, I remember—this is years ago, now, and the look on his face when he saw; not happy, not at all. A vegan restaurant in Echo Park? (Now there are probably ten. Plus a whole lot of high-end dining.)

At the time, when I saw his expression, I wanted to protest—as if he were blaming us. He wasn't. So why did I feel so guilty? Was it our fault the neighborhood had up and come? Should we apologize for getting in early? And were we wrong not to send him and his sister to the school at the bottom of our hill? Their educations in mind—not convenience, not politics—we'd driven to a different public school, a magnet, on the other side of town. And we'd only felt lucky and resourceful and proud for making it work; for sticking it out.

Having done so, I confess, it's lovely, bittersweet, to hear the clamor of kids (so many more kids on the block these days) walking down to the school in the morning (it's a good school now), and walking back up in the afternoon. Lovely, too, to have so many places nearby to meet for coffee—though, you know, you could just come over, since I'd just as soon make it myself.

20 COFFEE AND THE JEWS

During the Seder, it comes out that Maxwell House is responsible for the standard *Haggadah*—the most used if not exactly beloved. On that score, no Jew would go so far as to speak for the rest; what we're famous for is disagreeing with each other, about just about everything. Only check out something close to the original (not a more abbreviated version): early on you'll bump into "a quaint little tale" in which five wise rabbis argue about the nature of prayer through the night and into the morning, by which time they have to stop to pray all over again. I'm quoting from my own most beloved if not used. Is it the best? Not a chance. It's ancient for one thing: *The New Haggadah*, revised in 1942, 23rd printing 1973, talk about quaint, it's shocking to think we continued to read from it into the aughts. But you love what you know. Or you love your dad,[1] and the books were

---

[1]My mother married her second husband when I was three, and he raised me as his eldest daughter, as if I were his own.

his. There were nine altogether, hardcovers, packed and sent to LA well before the millennium, in surprisingly decent shape for the most part, only fetchingly stained with wine, soup, horseradish, unidentified schmutz.

Why send them to me? Because I was staging the holiday, that's why: Jews and non-Jews, descending in droves, including my parents coming all the way from New York.

On the day, Dad, who always led the service, wanted a quiet place to look things over. I offered him the deck off our bedroom downstairs. And I spied on him there, bent over the pages, marking them with a number two pencil— crossing things out—not just because the service was so long. *The New Haggadah* was offensive in so many ways: too much God for one thing—that angry old testament God. And all those ridiculous sexist remarks and asides (references to men's and women's work)—don't get me started.

That's why, a few years ago, when my brother asked if I'd kept the books, and, if so, if I wouldn't mind sending him one or two, I blithely sent them all. So I thought. Turns out I kept one—and I'm glad to find it here. Not that we'll ever use it again. By now, re the Passover meal, I've surrendered to the crowd: the shorter the better, that's what everyone wants. How long, though, since we had a real Seder? One for which anyone memorized, much less sang, the four questions? Or that song about the goat? (I can only remember the tune and the title—"Chad Gadya"; one little goat—not another word.)

Last night? We used "A Humanist Haggadah,"[2]—discovered online by friends around the corner—distinguished primarily for its acknowledgment of queers, as symbolized by an orange on the Seder plate. And such a long explanation for that—not obvious or logical, and not the point. The point being that most people—most Americans since 1932 (although this version was revised, at least, in 2011 with gender-neutral language)—have been using the one from Maxwell House. An advertising ploy, a way to sell beans. Buy a can of our coffee and you get a free *Haggadah*! Only in America (as far as I know).

The funny thing though (funny/surprising under the circumstances), there's no blessing for coffee. It would be really funny—hilarious and shameless, I suppose—if there were. But understand, in Judaism, there are blessings for everything, even the czar: that's one of the big laughs in the opening number of *Fiddler on the Roof.* Someone asks the rabbi if there's "a proper blessing for the czar." And he answers, "Of course . . . May God bless and keep the czar . . . Far away from us!" "Tradition," that's the name of that well-known song. And alongside the big traditions, every family has its own.

On Yom Kippur, for instance, Dad and Little Gramma (his mother) spent the day at the synagogue, a converted five-bedroom colonial in a town with a church on every corner, it seemed. They fasted, too, from morning till night. He maybe

---

[2]http://uuja.org/holidays/lit/Humanist_Haggadah.pdf, courtesy of the Unitarian Universalists for Jewish Awareness, who credit the Machar congregation for Secular Humanistic Judaism in Washington D.C.

came home to close his eyes for an hour. But she never did. Gramma, who lived in the Bronx and spent weekends and holidays with us, stayed all day at the Center, praying, davening, sitting with her back against a metal folding chair, her feet, crossed at the ankle, barely touching the floor. In the late afternoon Dad would join her there for the final service. Yom Kippur happens in October, usually, and this was back east, where autumn feels like autumn by then. By the time they got back to the house, all lit up and waiting and full of good smells, it was chilly and dark.

And we were ready for them. In the kitchen, a soup simmered on the stove. The table was laid with my mother's heavy silver; a platter of pickled herring; a challah, round and unsliced, wrapped in a big linen napkin. On the sideboard, a pound cake, or a Viennese plum cake, or an East 62nd Street lemon cake—some kind of cake, anyway, and an assortment of rugelach (tiny fruit-filled pastries)—and an urn full of coffee (Chock Full o'Nuts), of course. The aroma filled the house toward evening. Made you weak with longing, even if you hadn't skipped a meal. When they finally walked in the front door, Dad supporting Gramma by the elbow, before anything else, that's what's she wanted, needed. She'd enter giggling, giddy with hunger, exhausted and wobbly with having stood through the very last prayers—and I'd be waiting, towering, helping her with her coat, settling her into a chair. "Darling," she'd say, "is there coffee?"

And I'd bring her a nice strong cup (there really should be a blessing)—very hot, very black—and a jigger of schnapps in a pretty cut glass.

COFFEE AND DAD

Dad drank coffee in the morning only. One cup, as I remember (but maybe it was two), which he took with a teaspoon of sugar, and just enough milk to fill it right to the brim.

So picture the table set for breakfast: two placemats, two napkins, two plates, two pitchers (Dad's milk, Mom's cream), no bottles, if you please, no cartons, no plastic, no paper—and everything matching, the china, the linens—my mother sets a beautiful table, still; my mother is a bona fide chef, the original foodie. But Dad made the coffee. And Dad made breakfast—for him, for her (for us, too, when we were there)— his eggs scrambled hard, hers a bit gooey, her toast lightly buttered, his dark and dry.

Nearly to the end Dad made breakfast and coffee, even after the PEG,[1] when he couldn't eat or drink himself anymore. And he cleaned it up, too. Nearly to the end.

---

[1]PEG stands for percutaneous endoscopic gastrotomy: a feeding tube delivers nutrition directly to the stomach, bypassing the esophagus altogether.

21 THE WIDOW

"So Mom," I say (I interrupt) because somehow or other we have gone from talking about my children, their futures, their careers, to hers—and how her father thought she shouldn't have one; how it was unseemly for women to work; how people would suppose her husband was unable to support her; how she said, "Daddy, this has nothing to do with my husband; what on earth does this have to do with my husband?" As for that husband—with hardly a pause for breath and don't think I haven't heard this one before—he, likewise, didn't want her to work, and too bad: what did he think, she'd just keep having babies? Four children weren't enough for him? Did he have any idea how *boring* . . . ? Back to her father, lucky for her and her sister that they didn't have a brother. Had they had a brother—it's now that I interject. Because the connection is undoubtedly there—my mother does not lose track. She'll find the thread back to her grandchildren (who happen to be a sister and brother, *ah ha*, but the culture has changed and so forth, the pressures are different)—still, this could take a long time, and I called for a reason, I have something on my mind: "So Mom, this is entirely off topic," I say, "but remember the old coffee pot? The one we had way back when?"

"The drip," she says.

"It was a drip?"

"It was. It was made by Wearever. It had a copper bottom. Your grandmother had a whole set of their pots," she says. "Not that she could cook. She couldn't and she didn't—"

"Right," I say. "What happened to the pot?"

"I have no idea," she answers.

So I Google. And there it is—it comes right up—even though it's made by Revere Ware. Not Wearever. I can buy it on Etsy. For $48.00. And I'm tempted, I am.

My mother, meanwhile, uses a French press and has taken to reheating her morning coffee. From the day before. After breakfast, she pours what's left into a pitcher and puts it in the fridge. What she does the next morning? She sticks it the microwave. "It's just fine," she insists. "It's perfectly good, there's no reason to throw it away."

There's no reason, she's saying, to make a new pot. That's my mother talking, my mother, the aficionado of all things delectable, my mother who kept fifty years' worth of *Gourmet* magazines, whose own recipes (hers: my mother's!) have been published in *The New York Times,* who studied with James Beard and Marcella Hazan; who, per her questionnaire, is "very particular about coffee"; this same mother—her tastes as refined as they are—would reheat yesterday's brew? In the microwave?

This disturbs me so much—this is just so sad (do you hear this, Mr. Rauschenberg?)—how can she possibly . . .

Wouldn't my mother's day-old reheated coffee have to taste terrible, cream and sugar notwithstanding? Better not to bother with coffee at all. Have tea. Have a Tab. Can't she taste the difference, my mother of the excellent taste?

If she can or she can't, what I'm thinking she's thinking: it just isn't fair. She shouldn't have to make the coffee, it's tedious, it isn't her job; Dad made the coffee; Dad squeezed the juice and buttered the toast and scrambled the eggs—and then, for over fifty years, Dad sat down across from her at the table and together they began their day.

Four years since he died. It's morning in LA, and my mother is visiting. She's waiting for the coffee, almost ready, ground a few minutes ago, from beans roasted yesterday (Mexican Organic Belisario, with notes of dark chocolate, hazelnut, and cherry, and a very fine finish, and, no, I don't tell her any of that—I'm not that far gone)—

We've been talking about her life back east; she's trying to keep busy, she says, but it's harder than you'd think. I put a cup of coffee down in front of her on the table. She adds cream and sugar. "I know it's lonely, Mom," I say, sitting down to keep her company. "It has to be lonely."

"It's boring," she says. And then: she takes a sip, dabs at the corner of her mouth with her napkin and—wonder of wonder, miracle of miracles[1]—

"That's good coffee," she says.

---

[1] Another from *Fiddler on the Roof*, Jerry Bock and Sheldon Harnick.

22 ALTERED STATES

It happened again this morning—
Yet another person sent the Stein quote (the third to do so, maybe even the fourth), which, as it happens, I'd spent most of yesterday evening looking for; and it can't be Gertrude Stein, it just can't, or it must be a different Gertrude Stein, or else it's simply made-up and everyone touting it as if she really said it somewhere—and, as with Rauschenberg, this is a problem, right? All of us all the time quoting things out of context, and possibly getting them wrong? Ignoring (if not exactly on purpose) the original intention of the writers— not that Stein had any intention here: I'm saying I'm certain she never wrote this at all![1] But anyway here it is:

> Coffee is a lot more than just a drink; it's something happening. Not as in hip, but like an event, a place to be, but not like a location, but like somewhere within yourself. It gives you time, but not actual hours or minutes, but a chance to be, like be yourself, and have a second cup.

---

[1] Find this quote in her *Selected Writings*? I'll buy you a cup of coffee—better yet, I'll make you one, that's what I'll do.

See what I mean? Can we believe Gertrude Stein said any of this? Gertrude Stein said: *not as in hip*? She used the word "like" like a beatnik? Or a millennial? We're talking about *the* Gertrude Stein (b. 1874, d. 1946), the one who lived in Paris, the patron of artists, the author who wrote "A Piece of Coffee," quoted earlier, and here's another line from that poem that maybe justifies my mistrust: "A time to show a message is when too late and later there is no hanging in a blight."

Now that's Gertrude Stein. Said author Deborah Levy in a recent interview: "A Stein-shaped sentence is a very bespoke thing—you need an espresso martini to recover."[2]

Exactly. One thing to read *Tender Buttons* for the novelty of Stein's take on various objects—not only coffee (a piece of it) and buttons, but also, for instance, "Glazed Glitter," "Mildred's Umbrella," "A Seltzer Bottle" (the list goes on and on): another, to order *Selected Writings of Gertrude Stein*, because supposedly somewhere in that tome you might find she agrees that coffee "gives you time," and "a chance to be, like be yourself." That's so apt! So jazzy and smart! So readable and relatable and entirely *un*-Gertrude Stein—and to wade through the whole, *bespoke*, selected, 706 pages worth—

Well, I can't. I tried, I did, but I can't. There's not enough coffee in the world . . .

---

[2]https://bookmarks.reviews/deborah-levyfive-books-that-unsettle-boundaries/.

However, to cast further doubt still—look here, from a piece about Stein in an October 1934 issue of *The New Yorker*:

> Miss Stein gets up every morning about ten and drinks some coffee, against her will. She's always been nervous about becoming nervous and she thought coffee would make her nervous, but her doctor prescribed it.[3]

So it's not like she even had a happy relationship with coffee. Which Deborah Levy does. In her recent memoir, *The Cost of Living,* she writes, "To sip strong aromatic coffee from midnight to the small hours always brings something interesting to the page." Could that be true? My devotion to the morning, to getting up early, precludes my giving it a try. As for espresso martinis—there really is such a drink, involving vodka, Kahlua, and the real thing: espresso! But I wouldn't be up for that either. Cultures in collision seems like—or does the coffee mitigate the effects of the alcohol? Or—can it be? Do those who drink espresso martinis do so just for the taste?

That I might understand, whereas the idea I'm protesting is that coffee is a mind-altering drug. But it is, of course it is. My disbelief is entirely my problem. It's just how I am. As much as they scare me, I've never quite believed in drugs—or, as much as they scare me, I don't want to believe, that must be it—which goes to explaining why I ate nine hash brownies

---

[3]https://www.newyorker.com/magazine/1934/10/13/tender-buttons.

in 1977. Not because I wanted to get high (I did not), but to prove, I suppose, that they wouldn't work on me. I spent most of the evening at the corner of Grove and High Streets in New Haven, unwilling to cross from one side to the other, convinced I'd seen my own death in the middle somewhere.

More recently—like last year—I ate two chocolate-covered blueberries, edibles, a gift from a friend who wouldn't take no for answer. "Try them, you'll love them," she said. For a year they sat in a plastic bag in a tray on my desk. One night, on my way to dinner with Eliza and Kim (my daughter and her wife)—they were cooking for us, I was meeting my husband there—I impulsively ate both of them. Had my friend mentioned that she'd given me enough to share? Like with three other people at least? Maybe she had. But, hey, I thought—they're old, they're stale, and anyway (as if I hadn't erred in this way before), this stuff doesn't work on me. Fred says I was unusually quiet that night, though it seemed to me I couldn't stop talking. And on the way home I pulled over on Echo Park Ave., a block and half from the house where we've lived for thirty-one years. I was totally lost.

But this isn't a regular practice, obviously not, I'm not one to get high. As for coffee—coffee the drug—if I drink too much, too late in the day, I might have a little trouble getting to sleep. Then, too, I might not. I'm not sure, if I couldn't fall off, or was restless in the wee hours, I could fairly blame a late-night cappuccino. I'm more likely to have trouble with a glass or two of wine. But am I otherwise different for drinking coffee? We'll never know—I'll never stop—

If I had more faith, I might follow Levy's lead one of these nights and make myself a pot of espresso instead of flossing and brushing—but I don't quite believe; I do, but I don't; that is, to stay up all night for less than inspired prose or no prose at all? I'm not taking the chance.

In the meantime. My husband has just finished *How to Change Your Mind*, Michael Pollen's best seller about psychedelics as a way to excellent emotional health. He'd be game, Freddy would, to give it a try. I'm thinking about it, too, but I don't feel convinced—it's not that I don't want to change my mind, it's not that I couldn't use guidance in the act, but I don't believe. And also, I do. (Here we go again): What if something terrible happened? What if such a trip brought me lower instead of lifting me up? What if, instead of discovering or remembering what I know, love, and value, I forgot instead?

Some weeks ago I met a friend to do a few laps around Echo Park Lake. Afterward we got a coffee, a cortado each, and sat down on a bench. I told her about Fred—how interested he might be in tripping again after all these years—how I couldn't decide if I was up to a first time. Along the lines of why fix it, if it ain't broke. But how can it not be broke? Aren't we all broke some way, somehow? Shouldn't we be? How to call ourselves human, if life isn't breaking us, heads and hearts, over and over? I thought I remembered that my friend had used hallucinogens, and liked them, and used them again. On this afternoon at the lake, I asked her, how was it, how did it feel?

She thought for a minute. "There was this one time," she paused, and looked out at the water. "This one time there was a moment when I felt connected to everything—I understood what it's all about, I did. I got it," she said.

"What?" I asked. "What was it? What did you get?"

"It's this," she said, gesturing with one hand. This. Not really a lake, but what? A pond? Not even. A body of water, not quite a mile around, the freeway at the bottom, Aimee Semple McPherson's Angelus Temple at the top, and, just behind us, the Episcopal Diocese of Los Angeles. Lots of traffic going by in all directions. And down here with us, just yards from the street, people walking around and around, so many people, so many kinds of people; people with cameras, strollers, fishing rods, drums, guitars, on bikes, and on scooters; people in sneakers, people in heels, people half-dressed, people in mumus, in parkas, and wrapped up in blankets—and people in tents, too, mostly on the grass at the far-north end, unsightly, those makeshift abodes, but nobody's bothering anyone, no mingling between us with our fancy coffees and them laying low. And, I noticed today, with no small relief: the woman who used to sit at one of those tables closest to the entrance of the 101 (at the *south*east corner), the one with the scary blue eyes, who'd disappeared a while ago, was finally back. Without a sign—she used to always have a sign; either some version of "Get Out Of My Face"/"Just Move On By"/"Mind Your Own Business" or "Need 75 Cents For Bus Fare." Today, though, she was all bundled up and wearing sunglasses studded with rhinestones (so I couldn't see those eyes, but I knew it was she), writing in a notebook as if the prompt were to keep the pencil moving no matter what. I'd have mentioned her to my friend, but such a long story. Easier to point at the dogs as we passed, who don't need explaining, so many dogs, leashed, of course, pit bulls, poodles, shepherds, all kinds of hounds and mutts; and birds— ducks, coots, pigeons, geese (a few of which were honking like bicycle horns)—somewhere an egret and a great blue heron, earlier we'd seen them together but not, fishing on opposite ends of the same long patch of lilies, the pads only, but the flowers would be back in a couple of months; the lotus, too, would bloom voluptuous, practically indecent. And the willows— soon they would be green and full. I can never get enough of the trees down there: the leaning palms, the molting eucalyptus, the floss-silks so pink! So exuberant! And the oaks, the sycamore, the acacia, the mimosas—the giant pines where, toward the end of the day, the cormorants hold court.

On that afternoon—early April, it must have been—only the magnolias were flowering by the old iron bridge, which is gated and chained, off limits to humans, but earlier, a cloud of blackbirds had lined up on the railing just so. It was late in the day—chilly, gray, getting grayer—and the coffee was especially good. I couldn't stop thinking about the woman with her notebook staked out by the freeway. I was so glad to see her. I knew better than to greet her, to tell her I'd missed her, I'd worried (easy for me)—but I'd wanted to—

"It's *this*," my friend said again.

This. Yes. Of course that's what it is.

FROM THE COFFEE DIARIES #8

Sunday morning. Fred's out of town, and I'm in hiding, trying to finish a draft. I've missed two deadlines (for understandable reasons, for not-so-understandable reasons): "Good thing," wrote my editor a few months ago, "that coffee is an evergreen subject." Is it ever . . . Ever-green. Ever-growing. It's a maze, a matrix, a vortex—if I fall down one more of these coffee holes—

But okay: Fred's out of town—the kids have made themselves scarce—everybody knows I have to get this done—

Although Stella-the-dog is coming to spend the day. ("Mom, aren't you missing your muse?" asked Eliza, her preamble to wondering out loud if they might drop her off.) But the girls have promised she'll be walked and fed—I only have to keep her company. And she me. The thing is, they're not due for an hour, so I was surprised just now when I heard the door open upstairs.

"Hello," called Jake. Then something about how he wasn't staying, only getting mumble-mumble from the closet in his room, a pair of shoes, maybe, or a shirt, and that someone was waiting outside in the car—

"You want to taste something wonderful?" I asked, coming up the stairs, glass in hand. "It's only cold coffee, but so good."

Only cold coffee. Only from Kenya. Only touched by twenty-two hands. Only brewed a few hours ago. Only black. But wonderful, truly—was that caramel I tasted? Who knows, not me, I haven't yet honed my skills to the point that I'm willing to commit—but very possibly it tasted of caramel, yes. I offered him a sip.

"I have a coffee in the car," he said. Still, he obliged me, he's kind that way. Then: "Mine's from Kaldi. Have you been to Kaldi yet, Mom?"

"I haven't," I said. "Is it in Atwater?" Jake's subletting in Atwater for another few weeks.

"It is," he said.

"You know about Kaldi, right? Who Kaldi was?"

"No. Who?"

And I tell how Kaldi discovered coffee. Or his goats did anyway. How they ate those cherries, and got a little high—

"And the rest is history," said Jake.

From your lips, I thought. Amen, I thought, we're very near the end.

"Back to work with you, Mom," said Jake.

FROM THE COFFEE DIARIES #9

Coffee, because I can't keep going; coffee, because it's going so well.

FROM THE COFFEE DIARIES #10

My favorite time of life? Can I even say? Wouldn't it have to have been when I wasn't thinking along such lines? When I was smack in the middle of—of living? When—immersed as I was in *living*, it didn't occur to me to wonder if I were living well? Easy to claim from here that life used to be better; or else that it wasn't, but might have been, if only; that we would have done something different (better) with life, if only we'd known, *this* is the very best time. But what a terrifying thought—to decide at the best of all moments that that's what it is; that things won't continue to get more and more interesting. Who could live with such an idea? Who could accept it? We can't, we don't, we shouldn't—if we did, we'd have to lie down and die right then, wouldn't we?

See, the thing about a favorite time of day—you can have it all over again tomorrow. But to choose a favorite time of life—way to undermine who you are, who you love right now. So I'm saying: none of those other times were my favorite—or else they all were. That's what I'd have said if you'd asked me, and that's what I'm telling you now. *This*, this is my favorite time, it *has* to be. Not that the past is dead or even past (forgive my paraphrasing, William Faulkner)—but what it certainly is, is mostly evaporated, static, backscatter. As for what's to come, I can't possibly count on that—on anything to come at all—I'm old enough to know better by now.

This morning while making the coffee (waiting for the water to boil), I peered into the almost dark in the valley below and a light in a window snagged me. I was curious. And comforted, too—someone else was awake before dawn. In my case it's because I'm on east coast time, just back from ten days of teaching in Vermont, ten days of institutional coffee. So of course I was looking forward to getting home to mine, to ours—to the Trystero's—but somewhere between Chicago and Nevada I caught the most awful cold. The upshot being I can't taste anything this morning, not really. Delicious, Fred will say when he wakes (as always), but I wouldn't know. A pleasure necessarily deferred. Otherwise, though—here's the question I've been asking myself—why defer pleasure? Who would? For what? You get to a point in life (you have blue hair, this is what it's come to), you want what you want and you want it now: not because you suppose you deserve it; not because you're entitled or spoiled, though incredibly fortunate you certainly are—rather because you realize anew, for real, you won't be around forever, you really won't. I really won't.

But from here arises another question: what *is* pleasure? From whence does it come? If you believe that pleasure, joy, happiness, a sense of well-being, goes arm in arm with anticipation, well then, all right, deferral turns out to be not so unpleasant—not an ordeal. All the better, though, or possibly equally gratifying to think that embracing your certain demise might allow you to accept that whether or not you have anything certain to look forward to (other than *death*), look around: you actually have what you have, you are what you are right now. In which case, there's pleasure in just making the coffee in your own little house, in your own little kitchen, with a view that includes a little square of window below, a stranger's window, where, you imagine, the stranger is also straddling the past and the future to imagine herself into this moment now.

EPILOGUE

It's morning. There she is again, that woman in her robe, making extra coffee. She's been making extra coffee for a while, she has—I have—

Extra coffee for an extra-long moment; that's all it is, she knows that; I know that, I do—

Backing up for a minute:

Once upon a time, when coffee, like most things, was something to take entirely for granted, they got up, the young couple (youngish anyway—young on a relative scale), and, of course, they started the coffee, and woke the kids—who were always good kids, who got up, got washed, got dressed, ate breakfast, while the woman bagged lunches, and the man fed the dogs (or vice versa)—and then they piled into the car, the kids did, and depending on their schedules (car pool), one or the other, the man or the woman got behind the wheel, and off they went—to school, to work—and year after year this was how the days unfurled—

Until the kids went away to college, both of them—

And the dogs died—and, sidebar, this is my mother's favorite joke: a guy asks a priest, when does life begin. And the priest says, At conception, my son. Then the guy asks the minister, Father, when does life begin? And the minister says: At the moment of birth. To round things out, to be fair, for good measure the guy approaches a rabbi: Rabbi, when does life begin? he asks. And the rabbi answers, Life begins, my son, when the children leave home and the dog is dead.

The thing is, in our case, the children moved back from the other coast, what a relief (for the moment anyway, for the moment), into places of their own; and then one of them (the girl) got married, and the other (the boy) started seeing a woman who, what a coincidence, lives around the corner—

And *then*:

Then, just last summer, the marrieds got a dog. They called us in Paris to say it was happening. Two puppies left in the litter, said Eliza, did we want one, too? (We'll take care of her for you till you come home, she said.) Did we? I asked Fred. Do we want a dog? Are you kidding, he said, are you nuts? Trust me, he said—they're getting a dog, we're getting a dog, wait and see—

How did he know? But sure enough, the girls work full time, both of them do—and Stella-the-dog, who is otherwise the very best dog in the world, has separation anxiety; she can't be left alone—and who works at home, who can hang out with the dog, day after day, you guessed it, I do, I can, that's who.

So this is what's happening in this long-extended moment—which we will no doubt remember as a blip. No joke, when does life begin? Every morning, just before eight—that's when Eliza drops off the dog. Stella. Who, I must tell you, is never not happy to see me, because A) She's a dog, and B) I feed her all day long—

She loves you best, Mom, says Eliza.

She doesn't, I say.

She does, says Fred. You're lovable. And you feed her all day long.

But now here's the other thing. Jake is presently, in this moment, betwixt and between, and mostly staying with his girlfriend (the one who lives around the corner)—so it makes sense for him to run up the hill to our house for a shower and shave, a piece of toast, a cup of Joe—

The other morning, just after 8, there we all were, the original four plus Stella-the-dog—and we realized! And we laughed. And gasped. At least I did, looked around, put my hand to my mouth, I almost had to sit down, it was dizzying, it was time made visible—an optical illusion—the moment, the extended moment, expanding to accommodate the years in between, all of us together, each of us about to head out into the day, but first—

Who wants coffee?

(Amen.)

ACKNOWLEDGMENTS

Thanks to everyone who helped with this project:

Kim Adrian, Jan Anderson, Jack Arky, Johanna Blakley, Doug Bauer, Emilie Pascale Beck, Amanda Bestor-Seigel, David Biespiel, Sven Birkerts, Julie Callahan, Pat Callahan, Susan Cheever, Bernard Cooper, Meghan Daum, LeAnne Downing, Rae Dubow, Charles Fleming, Agatha French, Pamela Galvin, Susan Kaiser Greenland, Seth Greenland, Monie Hardwick, Craig Holt, Karen Karbo, Ariana Kelly, Dorna Khazeni, Lauren Klein, Didi Jackson, Major Jackson, Sonja Livingston, Tom Lutz, Maria Maisto, Michelle Maisto, Dan McCloskey, Jill McCorkle, Deirdre McNamer, Susan Scarf Merrell, James Merrell, Benjamin Mesirow, Tod Mesirow, Becca Millstein, Robert Myhill, Rachel Pastan, Rolf Potts, Sarah Ream, Sally Robinson, Carole Rubinstein-Mendel, Jay Ruskey, Lindsay Ryan, Marjorie Sandor, Erika Schickel, Marisa Silver, Jessica Silvester, Julie Singer, Dan Smetanka, Eulysses Spode, Kitty Swink, Jennabeth Taliaferro, Greg Thomas, Peter Trachtenberg, David Ulin, Stacy Valis, Teresa Von Fuchs, Diana Wagman, Joan Wickersham, Ross White (founder of The Grind), and Amy Wilentz.

Did I forget anybody? If I did, I'll do my best to make it up to you. Like last time, somehow I left out Tod Goldberg, so I'm thanking him now: Tod, thank you, I owe you.

Amy Gerstler, *I'll be thanking you always* (sung to the traditional tune[1]), for a zillion things, on top of which, there's no better reader in the world, lucky me. Lucky, too, to get to work with the team at Bloomsbury, including Leela Ulaganathan, Amy Martin, Zoe Jellicoe, Haaris Naqvi, Ian Bogost, and especially Christopher Schaberg and Anahi Molina who read so closely and so well.

I'm grateful to my mother, Leah Lenney, my aunt, Abby Selinger, and my siblings, Joe, Andy, and Jill, for reminding me how we used to be—

And to Jake, and Eliza, and Kim, without whom I wouldn't be who I am—

Finally Freddy—who else drinks the coffee every morning, and only ever says "delicious"? Thank you, love.

---

[1] H/T Irving Berlin. From "Always," 1925.

MY COFFEE BOOK FORT (FURTHER READING)

The north side (on my desk):

Uncommon Grounds (Mark Pendergrast) to my right.
The New Coffee Rules (Michelman and Carlsen) to my left.

The eastern border (on the floor):

A Tree Grows in Brooklyn (Betty Smith)
Out of Africa (Isak Dinesen)
M Train (Patti Smith)
The Art of Eating (MFK Fisher)
The Monk of Mokha (Dave Eggers)
Real Fresh Coffee (Torz and Macatonia)
Where to Drink Coffee (Clayton and Ross)
Coffee Nerd (Ruth Brown)
The Physiology of Taste (Brillat-Savarin, translated by MFK Fisher)

To the west (on the floor):

Hot Milk (Deborah Levy)

Treatise on Modern Stimulants (Honoré de Balzac)

A Selection of Dishes and the Chef's Reminder (Charles Fellows)

How to Travel with Salmon (Umberto Ecco)

The Blue Bottle Craft of Coffee (Freeman, Freeman, and Duggan)

The Measure of Her Powers (MFK Fisher)

To the south (on the floor behind me, I mean):

Where the Wild Coffee Grows (Jeff Koehler)

The Coffee Dictionary (Maxwell Colonna-Dashwood)

Mason & Dixon (Thomas Pynchon)

Selected Writings (Gertrude Stein)

Tender Buttons (Gertrude Stein)

Balzac (Stefan Zweig)

The History of the World in 6 Glasses (Tom Standage)

And a special edition of *Time Magazine: Coffee: The Culture. The Business. Your Health.*

INDEX